Critical Thinking for Education Students

Critical Thinking for Education Students

How to Argue, Analyse and Reflect

Charlotte Barrow and
Rebecca Westrup

BLOOMSBURY ACADEMIC
LONDON • NEW YORK • OXFORD • NEW DELHI • SYDNEY

BLOOMSBURY ACADEMIC
Bloomsbury Publishing Plc, 50 Bedford Square, London, WC1B 3DP, UK
Bloomsbury Publishing Inc, 1359 Broadway, New York, NY 10018, USA
Bloomsbury Publishing Ireland, 29 Earlsfort Terrace, Dublin 2, D02 AY28, Ireland

BLOOMSBURY, BLOOMSBURY ACADEMIC and the Diana logo are trademarks of
Bloomsbury Publishing Plc

First published in Great Britain 2026

Copyright © Charlotte Barrow and Rebecca Westrup, 2026

Charlotte Barrow and Rebecca Westrup have asserted their right under the Copyright, Designs
and Patents Act, 1988, to be identified as Authors of this work.

Cover design: Jade Barnett

All rights reserved. No part of this publication may be: i) reproduced or transmitted in
any form, electronic or mechanical, including photocopying, recording or by means of
any information storage or retrieval system without prior permission in writing from the
publishers; or ii) used or reproduced in any way for the training, development or operation of
artificial intelligence (AI) technologies, including generative AI technologies. The rights holders
expressly reserve this publication from the text and data mining exception as per Article 4(3)
of the Digital Single Market Directive (EU) 2019/790.

Bloomsbury Publishing Plc does not have any control over, or responsibility for, any third-party
websites referred to or in this book. All internet addresses given in this book were correct
at the time of going to press. The author and publisher regret any inconvenience caused if
addresses have changed or sites have ceased
to exist, but can accept no responsibility for any such changes.

A catalogue record for this book is available from the British Library.

Library of Congress Cataloging-in-Publication Data
Names: Barrow, Charlotte, author. | Westrup, Rebecca, author.
Title: Critical thinking for education students : how to argue, analyse and reflect / Charlotte
Barrow and Rebecca Westrup.
Description: London ; New York : Bloomsbury Academic, 2026. | Series: Bloomsbury study
skills | Includes bibliographical references and index. | Summary: "The ability to weigh
up arguments and make informed judgements is a skill that will benefit students in their
academic work, in their placements, and in their professional lives. This book outlines what
critical thinking and critical reflection mean in the context of studying Education or Childhood
Studies. It begins by defining critical thinking, and showing readers how to get into a critical
mindset. Subsequent chapters chart the process of critical analysis at each stage of an
assignment, including how to read critically, how to analyse sources and how to write critically
while also containing guidance on how to demonstrate critical thinking in professional life"–
Provided by publisher.
Identifiers: LCCN 2025011583 (print) | LCCN 2025011584 (ebook) |
ISBN 9781350466845 (hardback) | ISBN 9781350466838 (paperback) |
ISBN 9781350466869 (epub) | ISBN 9781350466852 (pdf)
Subjects: LCSH: Critical thinking.
Classification: LCC B105.T54 B37 2026 (print) | LCC B105.T54 (ebook) |
DDC 153.4/2–dc23/eng/20250602
LC record available at https://lccn.loc.gov/2025011583
LC ebook record available at https://lccn.loc.gov/2025011584

ISBN:	HB:	978-1-3504-6684-5
	PB:	978-1-3504-6683-8
	ePDF:	978-1-3504-6685-2
	eBook:	978-1-3504-6686-9

Series: Bloomsbury Study Skills

Typeset by Integra Software Services Pvt. Ltd.
Printed and bound in Great Britain

For product safety related questions contact productsafety@bloomsbury.com.

To find out more about our authors and books visit www.bloomsbury.com
and sign up for our newsletters.

Contents

Introduction **viii**

Chapter 1 What Does Critical Thinking and
Analysis Look Like? **1**

The need for critical thinking in our discipline **2**
Developing critical enquiry: forming 'opinions' and moving
to 'informed viewpoints' **5**
What does critical analysis look like? Description versus
critical analysis **14**
How do you think more critically? **16**
Summing up **17**

Chapter 2 How to Read Critically **21**

Where has the information come from? **21**
Types of sources **24**
Identifying authenticity **27**
Reading and digesting sources with more criticality **28**
Opinions versus arguments **34**
Habits for critical consumption of information **34**
Summing up **36**

Chapter 3 How to Critically Use Sources as
Evidence **37**

Organizing sources: why is it important? **37**
How can you keep track of your sources and develop your
critical thinking? **39**
How to construct an argument and use the sources as evidence **45**
Obstacles to analysing sources critically and how to
overcome them **50**
Summing up **55**

Chapter 4 How to Write Critically (and Evidence
This) **57**

What does critical writing look like? **57**
How do you present critical thinking in your writing? **58**

v

How do you incorporate evidence effectively in your writing to support criticality? 60
Writing introductions and conclusions 67
How do you find your own voice and demonstrate criticality? 67
Writing critically, confidently 70
Productivity tips 71
Editing writing and final checks 74
Summing up 75

Chapter 5 How to Present Spoken Critical Thinking (and Evidence This) 79

Session talk: developing and presenting critical thinking in learning sessions 79
Presenting critical thinking with spoken communication 81
Planning for spoken communication 83
Using evidence critically and effectively in your spoken communication 84
Techniques to develop the skill of spoken communication and connect with your audience 85
Overcoming nerves 87
Summing up 89

Chapter 6 How to Reflect Critically 91

What *is* reflection? 91
What shapes reflection? 92
Models of reflection 93
How to engage in reflective practice 101
Showcasing critical thinking in your assessments 103
Summing up 107

Chapter 7 How to Demonstrate Critical Thinking in Practice 115

Critical thinking beyond university: it's a core employability skill 115
Critical thinking in work-based settings 116
How to handle it when things go wrong: the importance of critical reflection on a critical incident 118
Critical thinking when considering career choices 120
Teaching critical thinking: the responsibility of nurturing developing minds 122

Keep looking through your critical lenses: professional development   124
The role of critical thinking for inclusion   125
Summing up   126

Critical thinking glossary   129
Critical thinking sentence starters and other language tools   134
Index   137

Introduction

Why critical thinking is important

Mastering critical thinking as a student of Education is a valuable step you can take to enhance the way you receive, process and evaluate information that is essential for your studies, and beyond. Your willingness to engage in this and grow as a critical thinker can make a big difference to your own potential for development.

It's futile to present a simplistic definition of critical thinking at the beginning of a book on the subject, because as you will see, it is a concept which has to unfold and emerge. Chatfield refers to 'critical thinking in study, work and life' (2018: vii) and 'being reasonable in an unreasonable world' (2018: 149), both of which convey the idea of critical thinking as a wide-spanning and important asset. As university level skills go, adopting **a critical thinking mindset** is not in the same arena as learning to follow referencing rules or structuring an assignment: it's a bigger degree of development and has the potential to impact upon almost every element of your life. A bold claim, yes! But we hope that even just the smallest amount of dipping into this book will enable you to appreciate this for yourself.

The study of Education (and related subjects e.g. Childhood Studies) as an academic subject is distinctive in that it requires **frequent reflection** upon one's own experiences of learning: past, present and future. This requires a level of critical thinking to be applied to both the self, and others involved in teaching and learning processes i.e. we need to look through our critical thinking lenses frequently and routinely as a student of Education.

Compared to many other subjects studied at university, Education students will likely undertake some kind of placement in an educational institution as part of their course, and critical thinking skills need to come with you into these settings to help understand the multiple, complex, messy and wonderful environments in which children and adults are supported to flourish and learn. Examining the self, the practice of others, and ultimately our own practice (perhaps as aspiring educators) isn't something that all students are required to do: it makes students of Education unique.

> A small note: most commonly in this book we refer to the discipline of 'Education', but this also includes related areas of study, such as further or higher education courses in Early Years, Childhood and Youth Studies, Teaching and Learning Support, and any other programmes related to these areas.

Critical thinking is also a key component of many course or module-level learning outcomes or competencies and the marking criteria used to grade assessments at university level. Students are assessed on their ability to demonstrate knowledge and understanding of key concepts, critically analyse arguments, make links between theory and literature and apply this to practice. **If you can demonstrate evidence of critical thinking in your work, you will be reaching for higher grades** and will benefit from more meaningful learning experiences.

There are other reasons why becoming a critical thinker (and demonstrating this) is important, which are outlined below:

1 Critical thinking … to navigate information in society

The amount of information available to us on a day-to-day basis is staggering: this can be overwhelming and sometimes feels like we are battling to find the 'truth' or know which sources to trust. Almost constant absorption of information from differing sources places demands on our cognitive and intellectual resources, and sometimes on our mental health. This becomes even more complex when you take into account the possibility that some information we consume may have been generated by the digital world itself, via forms of AI (Artificial Intelligence) rather than originating with a human being. Thus, learning to work with AI and operating as a critical thinker when encountering or using AI-generated content is an increasingly important skillset.

Developing critical thinking skills can enable us to **command control of all this information** – rather than letting it control us – so that we are less of a passive recipient and more of a proactive and selective consumer.

2 Critical thinking … for employability

The Chartered Management Institute (2021) refers to critical thinking as one of the top three skills critical to employability: according to employers, this is one of the areas where graduates need the most training i.e. it's lacking among those who have completed a university degree. It's often referred to as a 'soft skill' but don't let this fool you – these soft skills are the attributes you carry with you, elements of your personal approach, your individual qualities and characteristics that influence how you work both by yourself, and with others. It is estimated that **only around 50 per cent of students have sufficient critical thinking skills** (Van Damme and Zahner, 2022; Chartered Management Institute, 2021). In the same way that university education is an investment in disciplinary or subject-specific knowledge (i.e. knowing about your chosen area), it's also the time to accrue and 'bank' approaches and mindsets that will be with you for life.

3 **Critical thinking ... as a future educator**
Large proportions of graduates from Education or Childhood Studies courses go into teaching, or other related roles that involve working with learners, often children and young people. The responsibility associated with passing on information and **shaping the views of developing minds** should not be taken lightly, and it is the job of anyone in such a role to foster critical thinking mindsets in their learners, to help them achieve their potential and navigate their way in the future world. It's important to know about critical thinking and understand the approaches to, and cognitive processes involved so that it can be taught, promoted and modelled in classroom practices.

4 **Critical thinking ... for lifelong learning, reflection and professional development**
In our incredibly fast-paced, complex and everchanging world we need to be continually learning about ourselves and engaging in opportunities for professional development. Critical thinking can help us to reflect on our experiences, question ideas, learn from our mistakes, challenge ourselves and consider areas of professional development to empower our future selves. Often within your career you will be required to engage with continuing professional development. For example, the Department for Education (DfE) in the Initial Teacher Training and Early Career Framework for teachers (DfE, 2024) state that part of a teacher's professional behaviours are to **engage with research evidence**, support pupils to practice critical skills, and **enable critical thinking** through lesson planning (DfE, 2024).

5 **Critical thinking ... for decision-making abilities within your studies and everyday life**
Critical thinking is a key aspect of academic **and** everyday life. Within your studies, it enables you to explore and engage with key ideas and concepts, question, analyse and make decisions about valued arguments

versus fiction or opinion. In everyday life it empowers people to make decisions in what is becoming an **increasingly complex society** both in reality and virtually, online. Critical thinking supports active listening, problem solving and communication. It also supports social responsibility and the impact of ourselves and in relation to others.

Katz (2018: 1) presents the idea of 'everyday criticality' and Cottrell (2017) refers to the idea that we all need to work on developing our **critical muscle**, which is a useful analogy to bear in mind: when we build bigger muscles, we have to then work to maintain them, or they grow smaller. The same applies to our critical thinking mindset, in that we can't just engage in one activity and then expect that critical thinking ability to 'stick'. It has to be practised so that it becomes a habit.

How this book can help in developing your critical thinking

If you're a student of Education

Critical thinking is not something that just university students should be working on – everyone in society can benefit from a greater prevalence of critical thinking within their life. However, as learners on a degree programme whereby your work across a period of time accrues a final degree grade or classification, **evidencing critical thinking can help you to reach for higher marks**. As we discuss later in the book, evidencing your critical thinking in a number of ways meets programme and module learning outcomes which are shaped by the UK's benchmarking statement on Education Studies (QAA, 2025) which refer to 'critical engagement', 'critical capabilities', 'critical reflection', 'critical debate' and 'critical understanding'. All this **criticality** is something that will evolve over your time as an Education student. It's normal to feel uncertain about the meaning of the word 'critical' in the early stages of your degree, but your understanding of what it means in both theory and practice will become more nuanced and layered as your learning progresses.

> **What does critical thinking ask of you as a student?** A willingness to be **open minded** and a wish to develop and **continue to grow**. An appreciation of the wonderful ability of the brain and an awareness of your own metacognition (i.e. how we think about thinking).

If you're an academic of Education

We (the writers) are academics with many years' experience of teaching, advising and working with Education students and graduates. Many of the conversations we have with our students are about what critical thinking is, how they can develop critical analysis and construct arguments within their work while also developing the confidence to display a critical tone in their written, oral and visual communications. In this book we have pulled together all of this to provide discussion and practical activities to support students with developing their critical thinking. We hope that you will find these helpful to include in your teaching and advising with students.

Book outline: what's covered in this book?

Chapter 1 grapples with a range of definitions of critical thinking from both published authors and students of Education themselves, in their own words. We talk about why critical thinking is needed, and how to begin doing this, in particular, moving away from opinions towards informed viewpoints.

Chapter 2 has 'How to Read' in the title, but is concerned more broadly with the job of consuming information from the perspective of a critical thinker, to be more selective and choose the right kind of information for your purposes.

Chapter 3 looks at what you can do with the sources once you've identified the right ones: how to analyse information from a critical perspective, and managing the process of your own ideas coming into conflict with those you come across in your research.

Chapter 4 helps you to develop a critical thinking mindset as you begin to write for assessed work. It contains examples of how to ensure your writing is rigorous, logical, credible and reflective of the principles of critical thinking that need to be exhibited in assessments at university level.

Chapter 5 looks at other ways you might be assessed and asked to present evidence of your critical thinking, whether this is face to face, digitally, or visually using spoken communication.

Chapter 6 considers your unique position as a student of Education, where reflection upon yourself and the practice and experiences of others is a core part of your learning, and something you are expected to evidence frequently. One of the most common pitfalls here is storytelling, and we will ensure you can avoid this.

Introduction   xiii

Finally, Chapter 7 shows you how to take the habits and practice of critical thinking into life beyond your occupation as a student. It will equip you with skills and coping strategies to take critical thinking into your working life and professional development.

> **TIP**
>
> Oftentimes, we will refer to the companion text to this book, **Writing Skills for Education Students** (Barrow and Westrup, 2019), which is aimed at students of Education or related disciplines who wish to improve their academic skills. Refer to this text for detailed guidance on writing and associated study skills.

References

Barrow, C. and Westrup. R. (2019), *Writing Skills for Education Students*, London: Red Globe Press.

Chartered Management Institute (2021), *Work Ready Graduates: Building Employability Skills for a Hybrid World*. Available at: https://tinyurl.com/28y62yyd (accessed 6 May 2025).

Chatfield, T. (2018), *Critical Thinking*, London: SAGE Publications.

Cottrell, S. (2017), *Critical Thinking Skills*, London: Palgrave Macmillan.

Department for Education (DfE) (2024), *Early Career Framework*. Available at: *Initial Teacher Training and Early Career Framework*. Available at: https://tinyurl.com/5xbk2ubc (accessed 6 May 2025).

Katz, L. (2018), *Critical Thinking and Persuasive Writing for Postgraduates*, London: Palgrave Macmillan.

Quality Assurance Agency (QAA) (2025), *Subject Benchmark Statement: Education Studies*. Available at: https://www.qaa.ac.uk/docs/qaa/sbs/subject-benchmark-statement-education-studies-2025.pdf?sfvrsn=a859de81_3 (accessed 6 May 2025).

Van Damme, D. and Zahner, D. (eds) (2022), *Does Higher Education Teach Students to Think Critically?*, Paris: OECD Publishing. Available at: https://www.oecd.org/en/publications/does-higher-education-teach-students-to-think-critically_cc9fa6aa-en/full-report.html (accessed 6 May 2025).

CHAPTER 1

What Does Critical Thinking and Analysis Look Like?

Being critical means being thoughtful and analysing what you read, see, hear and experience. This first chapter will focus on what critical thinking and analysis look like so that you can recognize critical thinking and apply it to your own studies and day-to-day lives (e.g. when reading and watching news and engaging with social media). It's notable that we don't begin by presenting a single definition of critical thinking – it's far from simple to convey the complexity behind this concept, and way of being. However, this chapter develops ideas around the various component parts of critical thinking in order to help you become familiar with the concept, and begin to think about what this might mean for you.

This chapter:

- Looks at critical thinking and analysis in education, early childhood, childhood and youth and education-related areas;
- Looks at the differences between opinions and informed viewpoints;
- Provides examples of critical thinking and analysis to help you understand what academics mean when they talk about critical thinking and analysis;
- Encourages you to stop and reflect on your own learning and to think about being critical in your studies;
- Builds upon features of critical thinking to provide a definition at the end.

> **Beginning to define critical thinking …**
>
> Throughout this chapter, we will highlight key characteristics of critical thinking in boxes like this one. These build upon each other to convey the various facets of critical thinking, and a comprehensive definition which we present at the end of the chapter.
>
> To begin with, we refer to a basic definition that we presented in our first book, *Writing Skills for Education Students*:
>
> > 'critical thinking means engaging in objective, balanced and evidence-based analysis of an issue, in order to help us form sound judgements' (Barrow and Westrup, 2019: 33).
>
> Here are some of our first-year students' views on what critical thinking is:
>
> - 'Looking at both sides and analysing in detail';
> - 'Picking apart all sides of an argument and evaluating the main points';
> - 'Being analytical'.
>
> These are all important component parts of a critical thinking approach.

The need for critical thinking in our discipline

As a student of Education, Childhood Studies, or another related discipline, you're at the forefront of increasing knowledge and understanding about the lives of children and/or life-long learners. This knowledge in turn contributes to policymaking and guidance, which in turn translates into day-to-day practice: whether this is in a professional setting such as a classroom, or personally in the lives of those who are parents or carers for young people. We all like to think that the kinds of knowledge informing 'best practice' are robust, thorough and well-intentioned, but unless individuals and communities of learners keep questioning and seeking to improve these knowledge bases, improvements in practice to enrich and enhance the lives of children and learners will fail to be seen.

Many routine practices, approaches and habits we take for granted when working with children or in educational settings have stemmed from critical enquiry, and subsequent research. Research projects themselves are born out of reflective, critical thinking that asks questions such as, 'how could we improve …?' or 'why does this happen …?' Evidence suggests that structured and purposeful research around education stretches back to the end of the 1800s at the least (de Landsheere, 1988) and this is a product of critical, reflective thinking and enquiry.

Some examples of research and critical enquiry that have originated from the reflections of professionals, or the desire to improve provision for learners include:

1. An increasingly common practice in some school settings is the provision of nurture groups, or interventions underpinned by philosophy or nurture. Nurture groups developed as a result of the work of one individual, an educational psychologist named Marjorie Boxall, who was working in London in the 1960s and consistently observed the emotional, social and behavioural problems that were being experienced by many young children. This was problematic for teachers trying to support them in learning contexts, and also because of the high rates of referrals that were being received by other services. Boxall identified an absence of nurture and some basic early experiences that were impacting upon these children's abilities to have secure relationships and flourish in schools. Subsequently, she developed the practice of nurture groups, whereby small numbers of children established nurturing relationships with key staff, drawing on principles of attachment theory. This practice has transformed schooling experiences for many children who have subsequently been able to become included with their mainstream practices. See more details at https://www.nurtureuk.org/what-is-nurture/
2. Lawrence Stenhouse was a key educational researcher who started his educational enquiry as a classroom teacher, asking questions about classroom practices and curriculum development among other key educational issues. A key aspect of his educational research and practice was the perspective that all young people could think about their learning in terms of enquiry (e.g. Stenhouse, 1971). Following conducting research into the humanities classroom, 'Stenhouse's project gave new direction to the teaching of humanities in secondary schools' (Rudduck, 1988: 34).
3. Charlotte and Rebecca (the authors of this book) became interested in critical thinking amongst students of Education through the conversations we were having about our learners' experiences, and the extent to which we thought we were equipping them with opportunities to develop this key skill. We wondered how we could demystify a complex concept that seemed to elude some of our learners. This has resulted in the creation of this book which provides an accessible and practical resource for learners in this field.

ACTIVITY 1.1

Layers of possibility in a school situation

Imagine that you are a regular volunteer in a primary school, and each week you report to the school office to sign in before you are allowed through the security doors to your regular classroom. This week, for the first time ever, there is no one in the office. The school is also extremely quiet and there are no signs of any pupils or staff. This has never happened before.

What possible explanations for this situation enter your head?

- There has been an awful catastrophe and everyone has disappeared. I should call emergency services.
- Maybe school has been evacuated due to an emergency, they might all be on the playground at the back.
- Perhaps all classes are simultaneously engaged in very quiet work and the office staff are at the toilet.
- All children and staff are outside for an outdoor event, and they have forgotten to tell me.
- Maybe I am here at the wrong time, on the wrong day.
- Maybe none of these explanations are accurate and I cannot identify the reason for this situation.
- The consequences of this situation are that I might miss out on my placement today, which could impact upon my studies.

Perhaps you have more possible explanations, but looking at the possibilities above, it is clear to see that the ideas that spring to mind include;

- Worst case, extreme, highly unlikely scenarios.
- Feasible explanations based on your prior knowledge of the situation.
- Consideration of the implications and consequences of the situation.

This natural way of thinking about an event or situation we encounter uncovers many possibilities which the brain can present and work through in lightning-fast speed. Usually, we are then able to pick through such a range of ideas and dispense with those we know to be less realistic and consider pursuing or resting upon those which seem more feasible.

To do this, we will be using logic, reason and – crucially – we are informed by our knowledge of prior experiences which have created rules or norms about certain situations. The extent to which an individual is able to engage in critical thinking and considerations in an event such as this will depend on many factors.

Developing critical enquiry: forming 'opinions' and moving to 'informed viewpoints'

How are our opinions formed, and what influences them?

Often critical thinking begins with the recognition of an opinion or a viewpoint. As students of Education, you may well be familiar with the Ecological Systems Model (Bronfenbrenner, 1979), whereby an individual (a child) is in the centre, and various elements of the environment in which they grow up affect that individual, sometimes referred to as 'circles of influence' (Bradbury and Swailes, 2022: 20). The model includes the 'microsystem', the 'mesosystem', the 'exosystem', the 'macrosystem' and the 'chronosystem'.

The **microsystem** is the system where aspects within this have an immediate influence on the individual and the greatest impact (Bronfenbrenner, 1979 in Bradbury and Swailes, 2022: 21). For example, this can include family, friends and peers and the educational setting.

The **mesosystem** is the system whereby all of the aspects of the microsystem are 'interconnected' and the interaction has an impact on the individual at the centre of the system, for example the relationship between parents and teachers (Bradbury and Swailes, 2022: 22).

The **exosystem** focuses on the influences between the individual and the wider context. For example, school policies and the impact these can have on teachers and their relationship with pupils. Importantly, this can also include exposure to, or consumption of various kinds of media, which can exert a significant influence upon young people.

The **macrosystem** is the wider social, cultural, economic and political context that the individual finds themselves within. It refers to the legislation and political decisions made about education, welfare, health and society and how these can impact the individual.

The **chronosystem** is the period of time that can influence the individual. Bradbury and Swailes (2022: 22) give the example of the coronavirus pandemic and the significant impact this had on individuals, for example the incredibly quick shift to online learning instead of classroom learning.

We can think of the higher education student's educational experience in a similar way and consider the 'circles of influence' for a student studying an Education Studies, Childhood and Youth Studies or related course (see Figure 1.1).

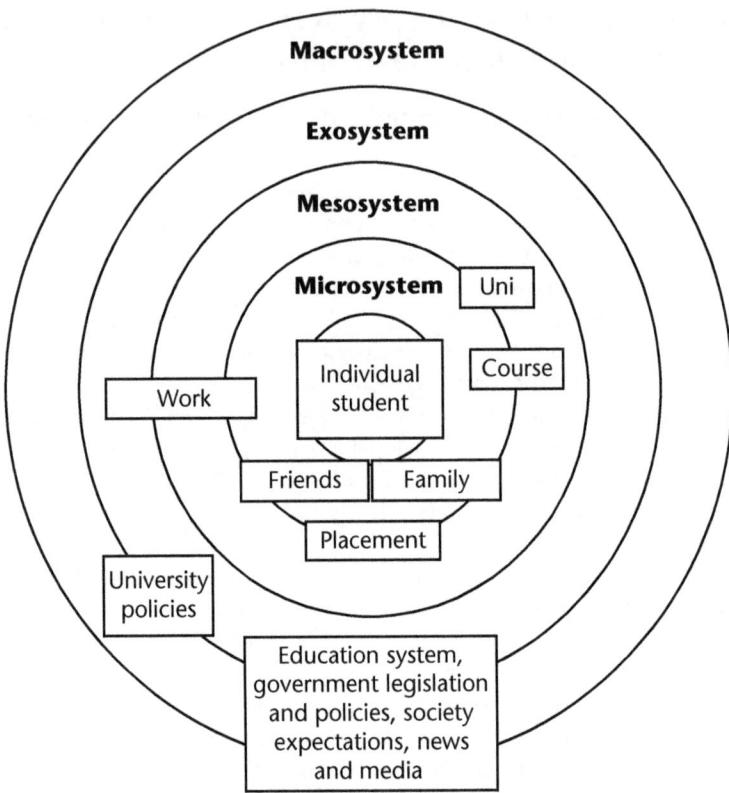

Figure 1.1 Adapted from Bronfenbrenner's Ecological Systems Model (1979) to illustrate an education student system

ACTIVITY 1.2

Reflecting on your experiences as a student studying an Education degree at university

Think about your educational experiences at university. If you were to draw a version of Bronfenbrenner's model with yourself at the centre, what might be in your circles of influence? What would you feature in the circles closest to you, with maximum influence? How significantly would your lecturers and lecture material feature? Or any volunteering or placement activities? What about books and journal articles? Would different types of media feature (include here any examples of AI-generated media)? Would university policies on assessments be important to you?

Use the blank diagram below to think about and mark up your own systems and influences as a student of Education, Studies, Childhood and Youth Studies or related course.

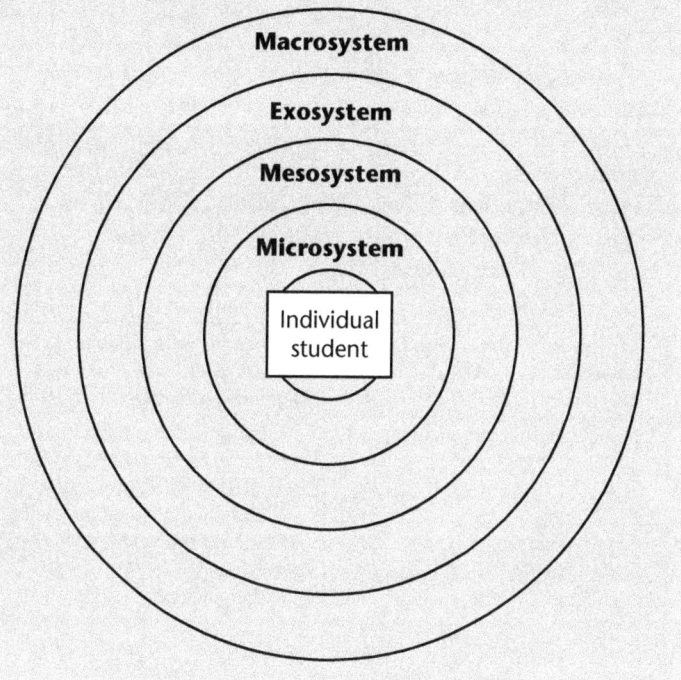

Similarly, the opinions we hold as adults are also informed by many people and factors. With this model in mind, while a young child has little control over who is in their life, and what they do and say that might influence them, you have the ability to be more selective about what sources of information you seek out and take on board. Being more aware of the sources you read or listen to, and the way in which you respond to them will enable you to strengthen your critical thinking skills. Once you have read through the chapters in this book (particularly Chapters 2 and 3), you may wish to reflect back on Activity 1.2. You may find that you think differently, more critically about what you include in your circles of influence.

ACTIVITY 1.3

Where is your news coming from?

We always recommend that students of Education keep up to date with contemporary news and developments in the field of education, whether this is with regards to stories around teachers' strikes, university tuition fees or early years places for children in nurseries. You'll see that we pick up and use several current issues that have featured in the news recently in this book.

The places, or sources, that we obtain our understanding of news stories from can make a big difference to our understanding of the issue.

Take a moment and consider, **how do you most commonly hear about educational news and issues?** Jot down some further ideas under these headings here, to help you begin to think about this in greater depth. We've provided a couple of examples.

Sources of news	Comments on this
My lecturers often bring current news stories to our attention in class.	Might they only pick up and present what they feel to be of significance?
I follow various news sources on social media.	Online algorithms can dictate what one person views and be selective about what to present to you. Media outlets online are all looking for the next 'click'.

Every source of information comes with a range of considerations, and issues presented in the media are always likely to be subjected to greater degrees of bias, subjectivity and motivations from those behind them. Being aware of this is a crucial mindset to begin with when you're committing to becoming a critical thinker.

> **TIP**
>
> Your tendency to engage in critical thinking may depend upon the people, community, media and aspects of society around you that you engage with.

The difference between 'opinions' and 'informed viewpoints'

It is this ability to be able to read, understand and select sources of information to take on board and use as evidence that will help you to **move beyond just having an opinion to being able to provide an informed viewpoint.** To help us understand the difference between an 'opinion' and an 'informed viewpoint', we can think of the two concepts at either end of a continuum with increasing critical thinking, as shown in Figure 1.2.

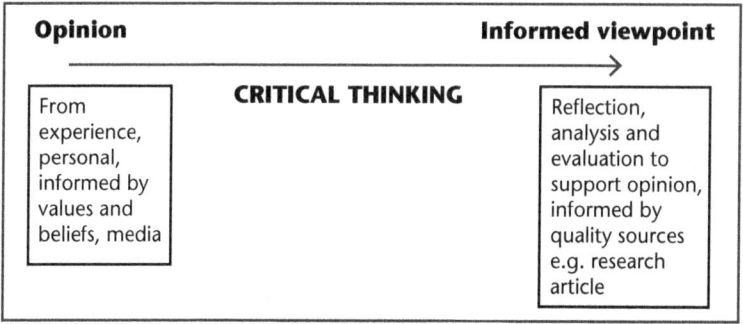

Figure 1.2 Diagram to show how critical thinking skills can help us to move from having an opinion to having an informed viewpoint.

Critical thinking and the actions of reflection, analysis and/or evaluation require us to ask questions based on our opinions to develop knowledge and understanding. A critical thinker knows how to move *beyond* opinions in order to progress and improve the quality of an argument.

ACTIVITY 1.4

Sources of information from opinions or informed viewpoints

Identify the various types of sources where you would take information from when researching an issue (see Chapter 2, 'Types of sources' if you're stuck for ideas).

On the spectrum below, place the sources in the position you feel they fit best in terms of whether they constitute information based largely on an opinion, or whether they comprise an informed viewpoint.

Opinion   **Informed viewpoint**

←───────────────────────────────────→

Think about any common characteristics or descriptors you could apply to those that cluster at either end, what kinds of words do you associate with each? For example, under the 'Opinion' end, you might be thinking about the limited view of an individual who has written a blog. At the 'Informed viewpoint' end, the idea of publications from researchers who are expert in that area might feature. Consider some of the reasons as to why you perceive some sources better informed than others, and what the consequences of this might be. We'll pick these ideas up again in Chapter 2.

Example: The differences between opinions and informed viewpoints

In this example, students have been asked to consider whether children with a disability should be educated in mainstream schools or special educational needs and disability specialist schools. One student gives an opinion and another one gives an initial informed viewpoint that is based on some evidence from reading they have read.

An opinion: *I think that children with disabilities should be educated in specialist schools or alternative provision. On work experience, I was a teaching assistant supporting a disabled child with their Mathematics and they were not given the same equal opportunities and learning experiences as other children in the classroom.*

An informed viewpoint: *Inclusive education is a complex topic that has received a lot of attention in recent years. One of the main concerns is that there is no clear definition of inclusive education. For example, Hodkinson (2016) and Florian (2014) suggest it's unclear what inclusive education in mainstream schools would look like. Teachers and educationalists may strive to be inclusive and to give all children the same learning experiences, but the environment may mean it's questionable whether this is always the case. Therefore, the individual needs of the child and what provision is most appropriate for their education need to be considered on a case-by-case basis until there is a clearer understanding.*

ACTIVITY 1.5

Moving from opinions to informed viewpoints

What are the key differences between the opinion and the informed viewpoint in the examples listed above?

Comment

As you may have noted, in the first statement the student draws on their own observations from work experience and makes a bold claim based on what they have seen happening in one classroom context: this could also be referred to as 'anecdotal data' i.e. based on a personal account only, rather than broader representative research. In the second statement, the student uses more tentative language e.g. the word 'may' and draws on literature to support their own anecdotes.

Another difference is that **opinions tend to be more descriptive, sometimes storytelling,** and as illustrated in the previous example, unsupported by literature. In your assignments and when working in professional settings and employment, you will be required to demonstrate your ability to think critically and to analyse and apply key ideas to address situations or solve problems. Informed viewpoints should form the foundations of this work, rather than mere opinions (unless you are simply asked for an opinion).

> **ACTIVITY 1.6**
>
> ### Spotting flaws in arguments
>
> This seven-minute video from critical thinking expert Roy van den Brink-Budgen reveals some of the most common pitfalls we can be prone to when examining arguments or evidence: https://tinyurl.com/27ktyrct
>
> Watch this and note down any key terms that you are unfamiliar with. Maybe you can think of ways you or others you know can fall into these common traps around ways of thinking, or the presentation of arguments?

> Critical thinking requires you to acknowledge your own views as often being opinionated or based on limited experience, and to move beyond this.

Lecturers may often use phrases such as 'you need to be more critical' or 'try to be more analytical in your writing'. To improve critical thinking, it's important to **move beyond description** and instead focus on 'applying', 'analysing' and 'evaluating' key ideas and concepts and 'creating' new ones. In your studies about Education and Childhood related subjects, you may have been introduced to Bloom's Taxonomy (Bloom, 1956) and subsequent versions (see for example Anderson et al., 2001). Bloom's original Taxonomy was presented as a triangle with 'lower order' thinking skills (knowledge, comprehension and application) supporting the 'higher order' ones (analysis, synthesis and evaluation) that are all important for critical thinking. Anderson et al. (2001) later adapted the model to include 'create' at the top of the triangle. Bloom's (1956) is often misrepresented as a hierarchy and has been criticized as learning is a more complex process than the original representation suggests (Ellerton, 2020). Figure 1.3 is our visual representation of Bloom's model and we highlight the key and multi-directional processes involved in learning.

Inspired by Frohman and Lupton (2020: 9), we can use the taxonomy to consider how you might develop and apply the skills when you learn about a new theory and apply this to learning. In the example below, we apply Piaget's stages of cognitive development to a learning situation,

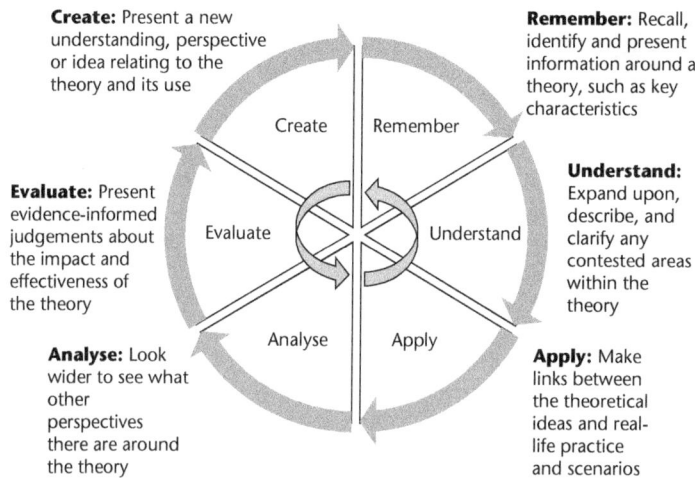

Figure 1.3 Our adapted Bloom's Taxonomy (1956) and thinking critically about educational theory

assess the learning experience and then produce a new lesson plan or learning resource as a result of this:

1 Retrieve information about theories or relevant literature;
2 Describe, clarify and learn about how the theories work;
3 Think about the theories in a learning context e.g. learning environment;
4 Synthesize learning about theories with relevant literature;
5 Assess the impact and come to a judgement;
6 Come up with new ideas to support learning.

As you progress in your studies, you should be aiming to move beyond simply recalling, or re-stating information and towards working with ideas more independently. This might look like being secure in your knowledge of a theory such that you are able to see its application in practice while on a placement, and then begin to reflect upon and evaluate the policy in real life.

It's important, however, to highlight that the year of study will determine what you're required to do. For example, although your lecturers will always encourage and support you to think critically and to evaluate and create new ideas, **you'll be learning, developing and refining these skills throughout your degree** ready for future employment or further study.

> **ACTIVITY 1.7**
>
> **Applying the categories of Bloom's Revised Taxonomy to the learning context of an Education student**
>
> How aware are you of the ways in which you engage with a learning process? Think of a topic area that is related to an educational issue you have learned about on your course. Reflect on your learning and consider how you can apply the categories of Bloom's Revised Taxonomy to this. For example, what did you need to remember? Can you explain the key theory (or theories) and then apply that theory to an educational practice context?

What does critical analysis look like? Description versus critical analysis

Common feedback from lecturers on work (particularly at higher levels of study i.e. in the second and third year of a degree) will encourage you to be 'less descriptive' or to avoid 'superficial' level discussions. Work that relies heavily on description and presents a lot of surface-level points is never going to enable you to reach for higher marks or progress your understanding.

When we limit ourselves to description, we risk falling into a storytelling mode which often supplies too much minute detail and can easily become conversational, anecdotal and too personal or opinionated. Purely describing what a researcher did, or what policy developments have occurred over the years doesn't give you the opportunity to showcase your critical thinking skills: it simply shows that you can rewrite, repeat – or even worse, potentially copy (and therefore plagiarize) information you have found within a source.

> Critical thinking cannot be demonstrated through pure description or storytelling.

In contrast, **a critical and analytical approach enables us to apply an enquiring lens** and often supplies us with more questions than answers, or reveals **complexity rather than simplicity**: these are positive results and all help contribute further to our understanding of an issue.

Critical Thinking and Analysis 15

> **ACTIVITY 1.8**
>
> ### Describing, then analysing a routine study task
>
> Think of a fairly routine task for yourself as a student: searching for a source within your university's online library. First, write about this **descriptively** (e.g. first I log onto university systems and then I …).
>
> Next, have a go at writing it with some **critical analysis**. (Prompt: Consider explaining *why* you undertake some particular actions, *how* you know the way to go about this, *what* you are looking out for, and any reasons as to *why* the search may or may not return the results you were hoping for.)

Do you think you could explain the thought processes involved in moving from description to analysis in the activity above? Consider what you, the writer, have done in order to get to this point of analysis rather than surface-level description.

Now try extending this to a more challenging piece of writing in the next activity.

> **ACTIVITY 1.9**
>
> ### Describing then analysing a learning theory
>
> Identify a common learning theory that you've come across in your studies. If you're stuck, or haven't had the opportunity to discover many theories yet, there is a good overview of core theories of learning that you can look through here: https://www.open.edu/openlearn/education-development/secondary-learning/content-section-2
>
> Select a theory and, once again, write about it descriptively, then rewrite what you know about this with some critical analysis.

Comment

Undoubtedly, it is more difficult to write about a learning theory than your experience of searching for a source in the library. Perhaps you noticed that you started to pass comment or judgement upon elements of the theory and the ideas behind it. Maybe you thought about its origin, who the theorists were and the significance of this.

Some core ideas to apply in this instance to assist with critically analysing the material (the theory you chose) include:

- Recognizing the strengths and limitations of the theory.
- Considering key features of the theory in relation to other theories.
- Exploring the implications for practice.
- Considering what alternative ways there might be to think about approaches to learning.

To substantiate these points and offer a robust critical analysis, these points of discussion would need linking to relevant sources to justify and add weight to your claims. Be cautious of claims provided without any supporting evidence, such as anecdotal evidence or evidence that is showing bias to only a particular perspective or not from valid academic sources. We'll look more at this in Chapter 2.

How do you think more critically?

Now that we've discussed what critical thinking and analysis look like and you have given some more thought to your own learning processes, we will focus on how you can think more critically and illustrate your critical and analytical voice in your studies either through reading and making notes, discussion in class and presentations and written work. Before we go into greater detail in the chapters which follow, we will look at asking critical questions, which are the gateway to critical thinking practice.

Asking critical questions

Being able to ask critical questions is a skill that is central to all your studies. As we mentioned in earlier sections of this chapter, **critical questioning is the beginning of enquiry** – it helps us to explore 'why?', 'how?' and 'in what ways?', and through questions like these we can make improvements in educational contexts. For example, when you're spending time in settings undertaking work placements, you'll be asking 'how' processes work, 'why' do things happen in this way and 'evaluating' whether they can be improved and again asking 'how'. You will also ask critical questions when you reflect on placement experiences (see Chapters 6 and 7).

> **TIP**
>
> Critical thinking can be prompted by habitually asking questions to create enquiry.

How do we create critical questions?

A good starting point, and one with which you might be familiar, is to think of Who, What, When, Where, Why – and How.

For example, here are some good critical questions to ask yourself about both everyday situations, and information you come across in your studies:

1 *How* do we know this thing, or 'fact'?
2 *Who* might disagree with this, and why?
3 *Why* does this issue matter?
4 *Which* people, or groups of people in society would be affected by this issue?
5 *What* could be the consequences of this issue or problem?
6 *When* do people, or groups of people need support in relation to this issue?

> **ACTIVITY 1.10**
>
> **Critical thinking checker**
>
> Flex your critical thinking muscles and ability to spot a weak argument with this short quiz by critical thinking expert Tom Chatfield: https://tinyurl.com/2y7dpype
>
> There's also a good visual explainer of how to generate critical thinking approaches in this useful document from Plymouth University: https://learnhigher.ac.uk/wp-content/uploads/Critical_Thinking1.pdf
>
> You could further develop your toolbox of critical thinking questions by asking AI to generate some as a starting point for you. Does it identify any areas to consider that we've missed out in this book so far?

Summing up

Being a critical thinker and taking an analytical approach to your studies and professional practice **is fundamental to your success**. When you think critically about your own practices, whether it's about what and how you're learning in your studies or in professional settings, you can articulate the decisions you made and why you made them, reflect on your learning experiences, evaluate them and create new ways to develop learning further.

> ### Defining critical thinking ...
>
> Throughout the chapter we've identified a number of characteristics of critical thinking, which are presented again below. Re-read these, and then read the definition of critical thinking we provide afterwards.
>
> Your tendency to engage in critical thinking may depend upon the people, community, media and aspects of society around you that you engage with.
>
> Critical thinking requires you to acknowledge your own views as often being opinionated or based on limited experience, and to move beyond this.
>
> Critical thinking cannot be demonstrated through pure description or storytelling.
>
> Critical thinking can be prompted by habitually asking questions to create enquiry.
>
> We asked some 3rd year Education students to share with us their thoughts about what it means to be a critical thinker. You can see some development in the reach of the idea, and recognition of the complexity of critical thinking compared to the views from 1st years at the beginning of this chapter.
>
> - 'it requires analysis of evidence – which also requires evaluating itself'
> - 'you need to be systematic and approach tasks and work step-by-step'
> - 'not accepting the first source you find, looking for peer-reviewed literature is always going to be better'
> - 'retaining your sense of self and avoiding too much influence from media'
> - 'really engaging with an issue to reflect upon it from an informed point of view'
>
> Therefore, when we refer to critical thinking throughout this book, this is the definition we are drawing upon:
>
> **Critical thinking is the act of seeking to understand an issue or situation through the use of credible evidence, which is then subjected to rigorous and well-informed analysis in order to present a logical, well-reasoned, and evidence-based judgement.**

A useful overview of critical thinking to consolidate some of the ideas in this chapter can be seen in this short video from the BBC and The Open University: https://tinyurl.com/yj7rewkx

In the chapters which follow, we will take you through how to read critically, how to analyse and utilize sources effectively, how to write with your own critical voice and how to reflect critically and demonstrate critical thinking in practice to support you in your day-to-day studies and professional practice.

References

Anderson, L.W. (ed.), Krathwohl, D.R. (ed.), Airasian, P.W., Cruikshank, K.A., Mayer, R.E., Pintrich, P.R., Raths, J. and Wittrock, M.C. (2001), *A Taxonomy for Learning, Teaching, and Assessing: A Revision of Bloom's Taxonomy of Educational Objectives* (complete edition), New York: Longman.

Bloom, B. (ed.) (1956), *Taxonomy of Educational Objectives, Book 1: Cognitive Domain*, London: Longman.

Bradbury, A. and Swailes, R. (2022), *Early Childhood Theories*, London: Learning Matters and SAGE.

Bronfenbrenner, U. (1979), *The Ecology of Human Development: Experiments by Nature and Design*, Boston, MA: Harvard University Press.

De Landsheere, G. (1988), 'History of Educational Research', in J.P. Keeves (ed.), *Educational Research, Methodology and Measurement*, 8–15, Oxford: Pergamon.

Ellerton, P. (2020), *The End of Bloom's Taxonomy: Why Thinking of Cognition as a Hierarchy Does More Harm Than Good*. Available at: https://tinyurl.com/5n85jmue (accessed 20 February 2025).

Frohman, R. and Lupton, K. (2020), *Critical Thinking for Nursing, Health and Social Care*, London: Red Globe Press.

Greenfield, P. M., Keller, H., Fuligni, A. and Maynard, A. (2003), 'Cultural Pathways through Universal Development', *Annual Review of Psychology*, 54: 461–90.

Rudduck, J. (1988), 'Changing the world of the classroom by understanding it: A review of some aspects of the work of Lawrence Stenhouse', *Journal of Curriculum and Supervision*, 4: 30–42.

Stenhouse, L. (1971), 'The Humanities Curriculum Project: The Rationale', *Theory into Practice*, 10 (3): 154–62.

CHAPTER 2

How to Read Critically

Much of the 'work' of a student involves identifying and assessing information, and this is often via reading text, but can also be more broadly in the form of **consuming information** from other media too, which could be in visual or audio format. For example, in our field of Education this could include videos, infographics, posters, graphs or charts, podcasts, TV programmes, or recordings of various types. One of the fundamental cornerstones of critical thinking is **evaluating** the kinds of evidence you are using, and so this requires scrutinizing and making judgements about the different elements of a source you may be accessing and using.

This chapter will:

- Enable you to approach your reading – or interpretation and use of information from sources – with an informed perspective.
- Identify and take into account a range of issues relating to the agenda or purpose of a source, the expertise of those producing it, and the reliability of claims made.
- Consider ways in which you can make your reading – or consumption – of various kinds of information more critical.

Where has the information come from?

The provenance of a source (where it has come from) is always a good starting point. A good critical thinker acts as a gatekeeper before even engaging with a source, and certainly considers a number of issues before investing time in reading and using that source – this is a process of purposeful evaluation (which is a critical thinking process).

Consider: is the source in question worthy of you spending your time on it? The questions below might help you to make this judgement.

How and where did you find it?

The easiest to find or first source at the top of the list is not necessarily the best. Oftentimes, a more thorough search using specific and precise keywords (usually within library search engines) will supply us with much more relevant information.

Who, or what, is the author or creator?

Take a moment for a little detective work: who is the author? Does the available information about them suggest that they are knowledgeable in this area, with qualifications, professional accreditations or other publications? A high number of followers, likes, ratings or views is not always an indicator that this is a quality source to use.

> Bear in mind that there is always the possibility that information you find online may have been partly or wholly artificially generated, and this can be significant in terms of its credibility. A quick illustration of this can be seen if you search online for 'AI-generated image of a teacher'. Do you see much diversity or representation of realistic teachers in these images?

What is their motivation for sharing this information?

Even seemingly unbiased individuals or organizations have reasons for sharing information and wanting you to access this.

For example, you might be looking for information about children who are excluded from school, and your research identifies the source types below. Note the differing motivations for publishing and sharing the information that might be at play:

Source ...	Their motivation may include ...
A local authority website – stating their approach and policy for excluded children.	Demonstrating their compliance with legislation.
A primary school prospectus – making public their behaviour policy and ethos.	To attract more parents to send children to their school.
A blog piece by a university academic – an analysis of recent trends in literature and other data types.	To enhance their own profile in the name of career progression.
A popular podcast – highlighting the experiences of pupils excluded from the education system.	To increase the number of listeners so that they get offered more lucrative sponsorship by companies.

Source ...	Their motivation may include ...
An individual parents' blog – sharing their children's story and the personal impact of exclusion.	The need to feel heard, connect with other parents, or attract media attention to highlight their case. Income generated for them by visitors to their website via advertising.

No author or content creator is without motivation, and some of the comments in the column on the right could be deemed as a little cynical: but some motivations to share information might significantly impact upon what they are presenting to you. Any issue or topic is akin to a three-dimensional shape: you can look underneath it, from above to get an aerial view, peek behind it, zoom closer then further away – each view may be very different.

> **TIP**
>
> The author of a source may only choose to show you one side of the issue – it's your job then to seek out perspectives that give you a 360-degree insight and understanding.

Where has it been published or hosted, and what was the process in the work being created?

As we cover in greater depth further on in this chapter, you may be aware that different types of sources are subject to different levels and **types of scrutiny**. Reviews, checks and editing processes are the hallmarks of sources that are likely to be of better quality, because the efforts that have been undertaken can go some way to **mitigate bias, objectivity and motivations** that are not always in the interest of the audience receiving the information.

With information you find online, check the host website/ organization – who are they? What is their vision, purpose and agenda? What kinds of other individuals or organizations do they work with, publish or represent? Are they a 'single issue' organization with a strong emphasis upon reaching particular goals or lobbying others to change views and policy? Sometimes this is fine, and it's important to represent these views, for example, when researching early years provision in the UK, we might draw upon the knowledge of specialist early years organizations: obviously they have a specific agenda, but they are also expert in these issues, and we would balance out their views with those from other organizations as well.

In addition, when we consider the process that was undertaken to create a particular source, there is a need to be mindful that some, or all of its content could have been created via some degree of AI. Sometimes it is not apparent what the root, or origin of ideas are within a source. This is even more of a reason to prioritize accessing sources via your university library, and ensuring they are peer reviewed.

When was it published or made available, and could this be significant?

Sometimes the date that a source has been published can be significant. Your tutors may encourage you to use a balance of sources from different time periods, and the reason for this is so that you can share your knowledge of both seminal, prominent writers and thinkers whose work has been impactful and developed over time, but also demonstrate that you are aware that knowledge and understanding can move on. Sometimes the contemporary nature of a source can be really important, for example, when researching legislation around a particular area, there is a need to check if there have been changes recently. Take note of which government policy documentation was published under (i.e. which political party was in office). The significance of wider political, social and economic climates and events should also have an impact upon the critical thinking we apply when we are looking at information from a particular source. For example in the run up to a political election in a country, the motivations behind messages from politicians change significantly: their onus is upon winning votes rather than informing the public in an open and balanced manner.

Types of sources

The availability of a source is not any kind of guarantee that it is worth using: any individual can produce written, visual or audio content, publish this (e.g. make it available online) and make claims associated with this. Don't confuse the best **publicized** or most **widely available** work with the best **quality** work.

Some 'traditional' ideas about quality in academia are still important to hold central to your use of information, and the principles of critical thinking underpin common values held about 'quality' in sources. The main distinguishing factor about what are often referred to as 'academic' sources is that they have been subjected to a process that is known as **peer review**, meaning that the work has been extensively and rigorously reviewed by other academics who are expert in that area. Publications in academic sources are subjected to this peer review and editing process that reassures the reader (that's you!) that the content is much more likely to be valid, reliable and credible.

Below you'll see a list of many sources, with some benefits and potential disadvantages of each identified. Can you add some more of your own thoughts and ideas about the value of these? As you do so, think about what has informed your views on particular sources, for example, has a teacher once told you never to use Wikipedia? Have you heard the phrase, 'lies, damned lies, and statistics'? Encounters like these shape our perceptions of particular sources and may influence our willingness to use them, and subsequently our engagement with them. This is a good thing because it provides that critical thinking prompt in your mind: why might a teacher tell me to avoid a source? Why might statistics not be telling the 'truth'? Every type of information has a potential benefit and limitation.

Type of source	Benefits	Points to consider ...
Peer-reviewed journal articles	Subjected to scrutiny by experts. Usually published several times a year (contemporary).	Exclusive – often only available to access for free to those within universities.
Peer-reviewed textbooks	Usually written by those recognized for their knowledge in the area. Undergoes professional editing process.	Can become outdated quite quickly. Expensive to buy.
Research reports from relevant organizations (sometimes referred to as 'grey' literature)	*Often produced by experts in the area (e.g. academics working with an organization).* Often timely and linked to topical issues in policy and practice. Easier to distribute/wider reach.	Usually aligned with the agenda of that organization.
Government statistics	A source of central records. Referred to and drawn upon by many other writers and sources.	Not free of an agenda. Varying changes in criteria can make comparison difficult.
Professional blogs or articles (e.g. The Conversation)	Often written by experts in the area but written in more accessible language.	Not always easy to identify the motivations and credentials of the authors.

Type of source	Benefits	Points to consider …
Individuals' blogs (e.g. those written by a teacher)	A source of expertise from someone with lived experience of that particular phenomenon.	Not representative of all similar individuals in that role.
Self or 'vanity' published books	Can be in-depth explorations of very specific and unique areas of research. Accessible – often print on demand (for a fee). Can be a great way for students (particularly post-graduate) to see their work in print.	Published at the author's expense (i.e. they pay). Some companies will exploit and pressurize the author. There may be little or no reviewing, proofreading and editing.
Videos (e.g. those hosted on YouTube)	Can share ideas in a more accessible way and add variety to the dissemination of information.	Can be made and uploaded by individuals without credentials.
Generative AI	Can synthesize a large amount of web content.	Can only re-present what is already available on the internet, and therefore is not free of the potential limitations associated with internet sources generally.
Social media posts	Wide reach. It can be useful to follow relevant organizations to keep up to date with news, developments and find signposts to original sources.	Can be published by individuals without credentials. May be promoting certain products, companies or ideals.
News (on the TV, online or newspapers)	It's important to keep up to date with topical debates and issues. Often accessible in a range of formats.	News outlets and owners of media are often aligned with particular ideals or political leanings – the agenda and purpose may often be persuasive rather than informative.
Conversations with individuals	Offer a great insight into the lived experiences of individuals. Can help to broaden our understanding and generate ideas we then take forward to research.	Only represent one person's experiences or views. Opinions can be presented as facts and generalizations.
Any more you can think of that we've missed …?		

> **A reminder on terminology:** when we refer to **'sources'** it incorporates all different kinds of media, and this list above demonstrates a wide variety of sources you might come across during your studies. **Reading** refers to the digestion and interpretation of information from any of these.

Although it's easy to view the task of sourcing information as hard work, here is an opportunity to reframe your mindset: as a student, **it is a *privilege* to be able to have access to quality research and to have choice and agency over what we consume.**

Think of viewing a menu to place an order: you don't usually choose the first thing at the top (like the first result on a search) – you go through carefully to consider what you would like, why, and in doing so there is a process of scrutiny, careful consideration and judgement applied i.e. there are certain factors that influence your decision-making process. The same approach can be utilized when reviewing available information to you: who is offering this to me? What's the quality? **What do they want me to do, see, think or become as a result of digesting the information?**

A key asset of being a student is that you are becoming equipped with the skills to be discriminating with the information you come across, and your ability to do this should be something to feel proud of. Remember to keep wearing your critical lenses and make good selections about what to include and exclude.

Identifying authenticity

As can be seen from the preceding table, identifying authenticity within sources is becoming more challenging due to not only the volume of information available, but also the questions we can ask about who – or what – has generated what we are consuming. Is it written by someone knowledgeable? Is it written by a human being at all?

> If something is **authentic**, it's generally considered to be genuine, to be real.

Generation of materials from various kinds of Artificial Intelligence (AI) need to be treated with caution as the authenticity of these is open to a lot of debate. The role of AI in academia is rapidly developing, with recognition that there is some value in rapid auto-generation of ideas from the internet. However, AI can **only** work from what is available online in a virtual world – and that is not the total sum of all knowledge in the world.

There's also emerging evidence that the way in which AI reproduces what it finds on the internet serves to reproduce the representation of inequalities and biased, subjective information online. In effect, whoever is shouting the loudest about something online is likely to be represented heavily in materials generated by AI – but the loudest is not necessarily the most authentic.

> **TIP**
>
> Your library is likely to have resources, and maybe tutorials or workshops to help you gain the skills needed to be a more critical researcher when looking for sources.

Reading and digesting sources with more criticality

When a source has made it past our initial checks ('Where has the information come from?' section, earlier in this chapter), there are further helpful prompts and questions to bear in mind when we begin to work with the source via reading, condensing ideas, taking notes or annotating. Some of these, below, help us to make further judgements about the quality of a source, whereas others are more focused upon helping you to consider how relevant and useful the source is for the particular task you're undertaking.

Consider:

1 How clear are the aims and objectives of the source?
It's desirable for an author to be clear about the intentions and scope of their piece of work – whether that's a journal article, video, podcast, blog or any kind of source. Not only does this further help you decide whether it's worth your time to engage with it, but it also acts as a reassurance that the author themselves is clear on the purpose. This is particularly important if you're reading a researcher's write-up of a piece of primary research they have undertaken. Without the author(s) stating their aims and research questions (what they want to know as a result of undertaking the research), it's difficult for us to subsequently make

judgements about how effective or 'successful' their research project has been.

2 The position and approach of the source in relation to wider bodies of knowledge
In academia – and many other fields – it is standard practice to begin the presentation of information by acknowledging what is already known about the area. This helps us to understand why what is being presented might be important, and how it fits in. A source that fails to acknowledge and discuss existing context and what is already known can be viewed with some caution: why the absence?

3 The methodology and methods used
When presenting the findings of a research project, the author(s) should clearly define what has influenced their approach to the research project as a whole (this is referred to as their methodological approach). Here they might refer to ideas and concepts relating to **their ontological and epistemological viewpoints:** complicated sounding words that identify the ways in which the author's beliefs and positions influence the decisions they made in their study. It is important to know this because this is the critical lens through which almost every aspect of their research has been viewed by them, and as such certain views or approaches will be threaded throughout the whole research project. For example, a researcher might believe in the validity of positivist approaches to generating knowledge, which value quantitative and statistical data (e.g. the findings from numerical questionnaires) instead of qualitative data in the form of images or words (e.g. interviews). A positivistic centred belief usually carries with it a view that the knowledge generated can be viewed in an objective way and generalizations can be made as a result of it, there is the idea that knowledge can be neutral. Other researchers (oftentimes those in the social sciences, such as Education) would disagree with this.

Becoming familiar with the language and ideas presented in empirical research (that which is grounded in experience) can seem like learning a whole new language to begin with, particularly as you progress throughout your degree and are expected to use more complex journal articles. A really useful body of knowledge to add to your critical thinking toolbox is to gain an awareness of the basics of research methodology, to help you navigate the sources you're using with more understanding.

Some recommended resources to help with this include:

- A short video from academic Helen Kara: Methodology, Ontology and Epistemology (https://tinyurl.com/52m62pw9).
- In the earlier stages of your degree programme: Chapter 4, 'Understanding Research Paradigms' in Williams (2020).
- In the later stages of your degree programme: Chapter 2, 'Theory and Method in Education Research' in Punch and Oancea (2014).

4 Findings, results, and claims being made

Every component part of a research write-up (e.g. a research report, or journal article) is related to one another. So, in the same way that we need to critically approach and query an author's intentions, methodology and methods used, we also need to **apply some scrutiny to the findings** they are presenting as having derived from their data, and the claims being made as a result of this. The claims made about what the data shows need to be directly supported by, well, the data! It should be clear how claims made at the end about the significance of the study, or recommendations for practice have come about. For example, if a study around children's friendship choices makes a key assertion that age is an important factor in this, then we would expect to see the issue of age featuring prominently in the data that has been presented, whether this is in the form of quantitative charts, or qualitative images or excerpts from something like interviews. If the issue of age is rarely mentioned, then why is it being stressed as a 'key' finding? Essentially, the job of a critical thinker when reviewing a piece of research is to check that there is some alignment between each part of the research project and to have confidence that the research is reliable and valid.

> **Terminology check:** Reliability and validity are words that are used a lot in relation to critical thinking. In effect, they are perceived as a kind of 'check' that is often applied to research studies, to further query their quality and credibility. Many would suggest that the application of these terms to social (and educational) research is now increasingly outdated and stems from approaches to older, more positivistic and quantitative research (Fraser, Flewitt and Hammersley, 2014). However, they are terms that you will no doubt come across, and are sometimes mixed up and misused, so take care to check your understanding of them – while also being aware that their use and meaning is contested.

Reliability is concerned with the way in which a certain phenomena or experience has been measured or captured within a research project and is considered to be associated with how trustworthy a piece of research might be. It is often associated with the words 'replication' and 'consistency', with the inference being that if the same research tools were used, but in a different context, or with a different group of participants, the same results or findings would indicate that the data collection methods, or tools used, are reliable.

Validity is concerned with the relationships between the 'test' or research activity/intervention and the results or claims presented. There is an emphasis upon accuracy of 'measurement'.

As you can see from the points above, these two terms are more straightforwardly applied to quantitative data. Qualitative research is a valued and common practice within the field of educational enquiry, and applying these terms to qualitative research is an area of debate in itself. A useful perspective to bring into play here is that 'Descriptions and explanations can be valid so long as one does not mistake local convention for universal truth' (Gergen and Gergen, 2000: 1032), meaning that provided we do not try to make generalizations from qualitative research, but appreciate the richness and depth in each unique data set as valid by its own accord, then there is no need to try and apply the concepts of reliability and validity to every data set, or study we come across.

In the next chapter, you will find an outline of how to create and use a simple Critical Thinking Grid: this is a good practice to help you reflect upon and capture many of the points raised so far in this chapter about the nature of information you are consuming.

Remember: to read critically means to not simply accept the information being presented to you on face value. It means making balanced and well-informed judgements about a number of characteristics of the source.

Types of bias and their impact when using information

The 'b' word is a big one when it comes to critical thinking. The term 'bias' is probably one we use in everyday language without giving its meaning much thought, but when it comes to being discerning about information we're choosing to use, it's important to know a little more about bias and the role this can play in being a critical thinker.

As much as we might like to pride ourselves on spotting bias and being a keen critical thinker, we are all subject to a range of biases, and these can play a significant role in the way in which we filter information. Our pre-existing opinions, experiences or knowledge on an issue can impact upon the approach we take. Do any of these scenarios below sound familiar to you?

- Being distracted by what you are personally interested in, or what just sounds good.
- Only selecting 'what fits' or what easily makes sense to you.
- Choosing what is easy to access within one or two quick clicks.

We are all only human, and our tendency to do the above is normal. Also bear in mind that information from some sources can be more or less susceptible to bias depending on its origins, and that AI-generated content is merely a reproduction of existing biases and representations that exist on the internet, and stem from the 'real' world. The trick to being a critical thinker is to be aware of and acknowledge not only that we hold biases, but also to understand the impact these might have upon our willingness to take on board perspectives that might be new, unfamiliar or different to our own views.

> ### Terminology check: Bias
>
> In its simplest sense, a 'bias' (you might also come across the term 'cognitive bias') refers to the way in which we might feel more or less inclined to align ourselves with, or believe, a particular viewpoint more than others – and that sometimes this might be an erroneous alignment. Having a particular bias means that we may then give overdue or disproportionate value to a particular idea, or thing, because it aligns with our own views and experiences more neatly and comfortably.
>
> It's easy to see here how the issue of bias is closely associated with related terms such as prejudice and discrimination, and the way in which bias is a core concept when it comes to the concepts of diversity and inclusion. You may also come across the ideas of a positive or negative bias, simply referring to whether the effect of the bias is thought to have a positive or negative impact (a judgement which could be biased!).

There are different types of bias that can come into play, the most relevant of which with regards to selecting and consuming information include:

Confirmation bias – where we are more inclined to believe a particular viewpoint because it aligns with our own. It is safe, and comfortable, and doesn't require any cognitive stretch for us. Chatfield refers to this kind of bias as 'the enemy of objectivity and scepticism' (2018: 11).

Conscious and unconscious bias – often referred to in relation to the way in which people may treat others who have different characteristics to themselves, such as gender, or race and ethnicity. *Conscious* bias is an open and intentional presentation of a particular viewpoint, with no reservations associated in holding a narrow view about an issue: this would be apparent in a source due to the very one-sided nature that fails to acknowledge or take into account other views and evidence. An *unconscious* bias refers to the views or opinions held by someone whereby they may be unaware of the impact of these views upon their actions, for example treating individuals differently due to a particular characteristic, or giving precedence to a certain idea. This may mean that someone is more or less likely to regard a source as reliable or desirable because of who has created it e.g. if the presenter on a video looks and sounds like you, might you be more inclined to believe what they are saying?

Recency bias – refers to the tendency of people to have more belief in sources that are contemporary and dismissive of older types of evidence: this means we run the risk of minimizing the value of older sources (remember that for the majority of human existence knowledge has been generated and stored without the use of the internet!).

Anchoring bias – this describes a situation where we are most likely to believe in or subscribe to the **first** view of a piece of information we have come across, and that, subsequently, we then may compare all other pieces of information to that first source we found.

A lot has been written around types of bias, and to find out more about different kinds of bias that you might encounter when navigating educational research, we recommend Chapter 3, 'Organising Your Research Reading and Avoiding Bias' in Williams (2020).

Opinions versus arguments

The overview of different kinds of bias above highlights that many factors are at play when a particular source of information is being created and shared. It might seem a little daunting to think, how am I going to remember to look out for all of these things in every source I find? However, as a starting point, it's useful to take a step back and begin with trying to distinguish opinions from arguments.

You'll find more detail about the component parts of an argument in Chapter 4, but essentially an argument is carefully set out (structured), has logic when presenting relationships and cause and effect, and draws upon and refers to (quality) evidence.

As we highlighted in Chapter 1, an opinion is a personal view or judgement that is usually based on an individual's experiences rather than a range of evidence or 'facts'. This means that claims about generalisability or representation need to be taken minimally. However, it is worth acknowledging here that in some types of small-scale qualitative research studies within Education, the views, experiences (and therefore opinions shaped by these) are held as valid and authentic perceptions of those individuals in that particular context, situation and time, and that they should be heard and understood within these parameters. So, opinions have a place, but the limitations of them should be central to your use of them as an information source.

When you're reviewing types of information, take care with the way in which you consume and use perspectives that seem to be rooted solely in opinions. The way these are expressed can sometimes be useful to look out for, for example 'Personally, I believe ...', 'I feel that ...', 'My view is that ...', 'My take on this is that ...'. Note that this is the kind of language you're more likely to find in sources or content produced by individuals with a motivation to share their content with you, and that these are not the kinds of phrases you would commonly find in most peer-reviewed, academic sources.

Habits for critical consumption of information

Clearly, there's no quick fix or simple rule to apply when applying a critical thinking approach to the enormous amount of information that is available to us. Awareness of the issues raised in this chapter should be a strong starting point for you, and some of the tips and actions below can combine to help you become a more critical reader:

- Never accept the first perspective – even if it 'sounds' the most likely, easiest, or aligned to what you already know about an issue.
- Don't rush your research on an issue – this will make you more inclined to accept a biased or most easily accessible viewpoint.
- Be prepared to have your mind changed – this is the beauty of being a critical thinker! What you thought you knew about an issue can totally develop and change for the better, which in turn will strengthen your knowledge and understanding, and ultimately the quality of arguments and analysis in work you submit for assessment.
- Ask yourself – what might be an alternative view to the issue you're seeing represented in a source if you were in another person's shoes, with different life experiences?
- Dig deep into the source – where is the author coming from, and why? What are they hoping to achieve by sharing their source? Is their work or content authentic and do you have confidence that it originated from people, rather than being generated by AI?
- Ask yourself, the 'So what?' question ... points and perspectives presented by an author need to be there for a reason, and a purpose, not just to afford them airtime, or to magnify an echo chamber (the repetition and reinforcement of similar views, closed to the ideas of others).
- When looking at a piece of research (where an author(s) has written up the results of their data collection), consider how different their research findings and claims could be if one or two factors in their study were different? For example, was the sample that they took their data from limited, or only representative of some people with particular characteristics?
- How well are claims supported? Remember that every 'fact', claim, perspective or piece of evidence contributing to an author's argument should be supported with evidence. And then you can ask questions about the nature and quality of that evidence, to further use your critical thinking.
- Keep careful records of the sources of your ideas and information, so that you can return to these and check, interrogate, ask questions and reflect upon whether they meet your criteria for inclusion in your work. This is also essential for good academic practice so that the origins of the ideas you present in your work are transparent, and clearly generated as a result of your own work and thought, rather than taken from another person, or generated by AI.

Summing up

On the one hand, accessing information is incredibly easy – there's certainly no shortage. Conversely, various types of information can be subject to many flaws and limitations and a significant part of your success as an Education student will depend upon how well you are able to extend your critical thinking to your selection and interpretation of sources before you even begin to work through the stages of creating a piece of assessment.[1]

We would recommend continuing to develop your approach to critical reading with the following sources:

- One of the many excellent OpenLearn (free) courses from The Open University, 'How to be a critical reader', available at: https://tinyurl.com/4frcfxry.
- Chapter 7, 'Understanding Criticality', in Williams (2020).

Note

1 See Chapter 6, Barrow and Westrup (2019).

References

Barrow, C. and Westrup. R. (2019), *Writing Skills for Education Students*, London: Red Globe Press.

Chatfield, T. (2018), *Critical Thinking*, London: SAGE Publications.

Fraser, S., Flewitt, R. and Hammersley, M. (2014), 'What is Research with Children and Young People', in A. Clark, R. Flewitt, M. Hammersley and M. Robb (eds), *Understanding Research with Children and Young People*, 34–50, London: SAGE Publications.

Gergen, M.M. and Gergen, K.J. (2000), 'Qualitative Inquiry: Tensions and Transformations', in N.K. Denzin, and Y.S. Lincoln (eds), *The Sage Handbook of Qualitative Research*, 2nd edition, 1025–46, Thousand Oaks: SAGE.

Punch, K.F. and Oancea, A. (2014), 'Theory and Method in Education Research', in Punch and Oancea, *Introduction to Research Methods in Education*, 15–37, London: SAGE Publications.

Williams, J. (2020), *How to Read and Understand Educational Research*, London: SAGE Publications.

CHAPTER

3

How to Critically Use Sources as Evidence

In the previous chapter, we looked at different types of sources, how to **assess** them critically and **evaluate** the kinds of evidence you are using in your studies. Once you have started researching, reading and gathering evidence from sources, you need to use them all together, and this requires another layer of critical thinking, when we begin to look at pieces of information cumulatively, rather than individually, and decide what we're going to do with the information.

Another key part of critical thinking is being able to synthesize, for example, to cut down and bring together, all the notes you have made from the various sources (e.g. literature, policy documents, podcasts and documentaries) and make **connections and judgements** about how you can draw on them in your assessments. You have found the evidence and now need to decide, based on your voice and the arguments you would like to make, how you're going to use it and whether you'll use it all or save it for another time (remember no reading, listening, watching, discussing and critical thinking around educational issues is wasted, engaging with the material has developed your knowledge and understanding and you could possibly refer to it in another assessment).

Organizing sources: why is it important?

Part of the challenge of working with sources is organizing them, as it is so important to keep track of which ideas you have taken from which sources. You might start off with good intentions, thinking you'll read and make notes on texts and sources separately and in a systematic way i.e. one after the other, but before you know it, you realize you have a messy and perhaps chaotic set of notes! Failure to be organized can put you at risk of being unable to accurately identify the source of an idea you are presenting, which can lead to being at risk of plagiarism, or academic misconduct within your institution.

How do you organize sources?

Students have different preferences about recording notes and organizing these and their sources. It is important that you have a system that is helpful for you. Here are some of the ways you can organize sources:

1 **An Excel spreadsheet or table in a Word document**
   Documenting and organizing sources and references in an Excel spreadsheet or a Word document can provide a resource which can be easily and regularly updated. For example, you can organize the spreadsheets or tables in topics and once you have read a new source with new information, this can be added to the document. You may need an internet connection to access the document and save updated work.

2 **Paper notes**
   Some learners also like paper, visual at-a-glance notes and to make these and update them in a notebook as they go. The advantage of organizing sources using this format is that you don't have to have a computer or an internet connection.

3 **Bibliographic and reference management software such as EndNote, Zotero, Mendeley**
   Bibliographic and reference management software enables you to make notes on references and store the information. You can also use them to add citations to your assignments and they will generate the reference list of cited items for you at the end of the assignment. Check with your university library and/or IT services about what software you can access through the university. Your university may also subscribe to other management software and have guidance about which types you should use (or not). It is also important to check that the referencing is appropriate for the requirements of your course. For example, if your course requires Harvard Referencing, you should check that the reference list generated adheres to this format.

Using bibliographic and reference management software can be effective for your studies as it can help you to save time: as the references are recorded you do not have to type each one out separately when referring to them multiple times and the reference list is autogenerated. However, if you are in the earlier stages of your undergraduate degree, we would advise you to also think about using a file in Excel or Word or paper notes to begin with. This will help you to develop a routinized practice with recording and organizing your references and notes on the readings.

How can you keep track of your sources and develop your critical thinking?

As a student on an Education or related course, you need to develop your approach so that you look at situations or issues from multiple perspectives and develop your knowledge and understanding so that you are not just drawing on one source of information. It's important to research many different perspectives to ensure that you have an informed perspective yourself. Bringing your reading and notes together and synthesizing this information will help you to demonstrate knowledge, understanding and critical analysis and thinking when you are addressing the assessment task brief.

A critical thinking grid (see the example on p. 40–41) can help you to bring all of the information together. It will help you to record the referencing information of the source and your thoughts and ideas about it following a critical reading (see Chapter 2). As a starting point, make a note of the following:

1 **Bibliographic information for referencing e.g. author(s), year of publication, title**
   This information will help you to locate the source should you need to go back to it at a later date. This is especially important for books loaned from your university or college library because there may only be a limited number of physical copies or e-book licences so you may not be able to hold onto them for the duration of your assignment. It will also help you to see the authors, or groups of authors, who regularly write about particular topic areas and the places they are publishing their work e.g. a particular journal title or with a particular publisher.

2 **Your own notes and critical analysis – also remember the page number for any direct quotations or paraphrasing**
   Make notes about any key relevant information and questions you have asked. Write down any direct quotes or paraphrasing which can be used to support your argument development (more on that in Chapter 4).

3 **Your interpretation(s), thoughts and ideas in relation to the assignment task**

In this column you should listen to your own academic voice and what your thoughts and ideas are. Some questions you might wish to ask are:

- What is the text saying?
- What is the text not saying? Can you think of any reasons for this?
- Is it possible to know if there is AI use? How is this impacting on the text(s)?
- What are the similarities and differences between the texts?
- Where are the connections between the texts? Do they help you to build a coherent argument?
- To what extent is there a connection? It's important that you can make explicit links between the texts rather than assuming the reader/marker can do this for themselves.
- Do the authors or yourself have any biases?
- How can you robustly defend what you've chosen to include/not include?
- What is your opinion about it? What evidence and reasons support your opinion?

You might also find it helpful to remind yourself of the checks we discussed in the previous chapter.

Ask yourself the question about how you can draw on the source(s) to develop your argument(s) and whether there are other sources you have found that can also be used to support your point(s). If you have a collection of critical thinking grids, you can look back over these to see if there are other connections to be made which could possibly strengthen the argument(s). The search can be across modules and years of study as well as within them.

An example Critical Thinking Grid

1. Referencing information e.g. author(s), year of publication, title	2. Notes/critical analysis Page number	3. Your interpretation(s), thoughts and ideas

An example of a completed Critical Thinking Grid

To demonstrate how to use the critical thinking grid, let's look at the following assessment task:

> 'Pupils in secondary schools should be educated in single-sex classrooms' – To what extent do you agree with this statement? Please draw on relevant academic literature and related documents.

1. Referencing information e.g. author(s), year of publication, title	2. Notes for critical analysis Page number	3. Your interpretation(s), thoughts and ideas
Harker, R. (2000), 'Achievement, Gender and the Single-Sex/Coed Debate', *British Journal of Sociology of Education*, 21 (2): 203–18.	New Zealand context – is this applicable to UK? Yes, there are similarities. P. 216 – the article does not support the view that girls do better academically in single-sex schools. Prior achievement and selection criteria have a greater impact on girls' achievement. P. 203 – highlights the link between girls' achievement, the 'myth' of single-sex schools and the marketization of education. P. 204 'Whatever the criteria for selection may be, it seems clear that the outcome could be much the same (for girls and boys alike) – the single-sex schools end up with a more socially exclusive group of pupils, whose prior achievement levels are considerably higher than for pupils at coeducational schools'. P. 206 raises the point that it is more about teacher education. P. 208 questions the enrolment patterns of boys and girls – useful link to UK research study Younger and Warrington (1996) – 'science subjects' are no longer exclusively for boys.	Highlights political, social and educational issues. Makes the point that it's difficult to compare single-sex and co-ed schools due to reporting figures available and flawed methodology e.g. not accounting for prior achievement. Quite dated?

1. Referencing information e.g. author(s), year of publication, title	2. Notes for critical analysis Page number	3. Your interpretation(s), thoughts and ideas
Younger, M. and Warrington, M. (2002), 'Single-sex Teaching in a Co-educational Comprehensive School in England: An Evaluation Based upon Students' Performance and Classroom Interactions', *British Educational Research Journal*, 28 (3): 353–74	P. 371 'Analysis of patterns of classroom interactions, together with interviews with students and staff, confirm that in many instances the single-sex classes support and sustain the learning of girls and of boys'. Not the underachieving boys issue. P. 354 'complex and multifaceted nature of the situation in schools (Kenway et al., 1998; Murphy & Elwood,1998)'. Highlights the need to focus on intersectionality. Exploring the long-term effectiveness of single-sex classes in a co-educational school p. 355 'through an analysis of achievement levels in the school at 16+ over the 12-year period 1988–99 since the introduction of GCSE examinations, and through a consideration of the nature of classroom interactions and the engagement of boys and girls in mathematics and geography lessons' P. 367 – single-sex classes reinforcing stereotypes and hyper masculinity for boys – no evidence in the study to suggest this though. P. 367 – Positive for girls 'Single-sex classrooms were generally construed by both staff and girls, as pleasant and safe places for girls, offering great benefits to them; they gave opportunities for confidence-building, enabling girls to be themselves and to explore the private and the personal, and to develop self-esteem'.	A case study of single-sex classes in a co-educational school. Methodology – analysis of achievement data and observations of classroom interactions. Link with Harker (2000) about teacher education and knowledge of different teaching strategies. Key point – it's difficult to say differences are just a result of single-sex classes. Highlights the importance of not just focusing on boys' achievement. There also needs to be a focus on girls' achievement too. Also an older source.

1. Referencing information e.g. author(s), year of publication, title	2. Notes for critical analysis Page number	3. Your interpretation(s), thoughts and ideas
	P. 368 'The overriding impression was that teachers were genuinely committed to teach in a way which respected both girls and boys'. P. 370 'the balance of evidence suggested that both girls and boys benefitted from having their own learning space, free from the other'.	
Clavel, J. G. and Flannery, D. (2022), 'Single- sex schooling, gender and educational performance: Evidence using PISA data', *British Educational Research Journal*, 49: 248–65.	P. 250 reports 'significant raw gaps' in single-sex and co-educational classes in reading, maths and science scores for girls and maths for boys. After controlling for an individual, parental or school-level factors, the gaps are not significant. P. 252 33% of secondary schools in Ireland are single-sex. Almost all of them are 'Catholic denominated' and there tends to be 'some degree of social gradient in the social mix of single-sex schools versus other school types' (p. 253). Quantitative analysis P. 261 the authors found 'no association between attending single-sex schools and performance in mathematics, reading or science scores for either males or females'. P. 261 'the results presented … are more ambiguous surrounding the merits of single-sex schooling relative to previous findings in Korea and Malta, but more in line with previous results from Trinidad, and so suggest that the impact of such schooling on education outcomes may be context-specific'.	Context: Irish education system and PISA data to explore single-sex teaching and achievement. Agreement with other two articles. Interesting to include a wider international perspective. More up to date perspective.

1. Referencing information e.g. author(s), year of publication, title	2. Notes for critical analysis Page number	3. Your interpretation(s), thoughts and ideas
	P. 261 found single-sex schools have larger gaps in achievement with maths and this could have implications for STEM-related outcomes. P. 261–262 authors highlight that the PISA test scores are not designed to capture student achievement. It also doesn't account for variations e.g. teaching practices – link with Younger and Warrington (2002) and classroom interactions.	

You'll notice from the dates when the articles were published that there are two older ones and one more recent one, a point worth noting. This was a deliberate decision made when choosing the source materials (see Chapter 2). The two articles published at the beginning of the 21st century provide a historical context and the article published in 2022 provides a more recent overview.

Using AI to check and reflect on your understanding

You could also use AI as a resource to check your understanding. Once you have completed your critical thinking grids and made connections between your ideas and the literature to create and support your arguments you could use AI as a tutor to check your learning, knowledge and understanding and reflect on the AI feedback. Some positives of using AI are that it can access a lot of information quickly, it can provide timely feedback for ongoing tasks and it can act as a proofreader for your work. Please note though, a weakness of using AI is that the content generated can be biased, incorrect and/or misleading. You should always check the AI output against your own knowledge and understanding, and other sources. We would say AI can be used to check opinions, debates and lines of questioning but using it as a source of evidence should be avoided. We would advise you to consult with your lecturers and/or your university's policies and guidance about AI use in learning, teaching and assessment if you have any questions about using it.

> **ACTIVITY 3.1**
>
> **What are the positives and weaknesses with using AI in your studies?**
>
> In the previous paragraph we have started to consider the benefits and limitations with using AI in your studies. Can you think of any others? Complete the table below.
>
> | Benefits of using AI in your studies | Limitations of using AI in your studies |
> |---|---|
> | Access to a lot of information | Some of the information is made up |
> | Provides timely feedback | The information could be biased |

How to construct an argument and use the sources as evidence

Now that you've decided what evidence from a range of sources (e.g. literature, podcasts, policy documents and documentaries) to include in an assessment to support your points, you need to consider what you would like to say and what the argument is going to look like.

Building your argument: supporting your claims

Once you have decided on your argument and developing line of the argument you need to demonstrate, illustrate and support it with evidence from relevant literature and wider reading. As Birrell Ivory (2021) notes, it's important to look at all of the evidence you have compiled from your critical reading and critical thinking about this to decide what your answer or response is. The argument development process requires critical thinking. Similarly to the critical reading process,

ACTIVITY 3.2

Freewriting what you want to say

Katz (2018) highlights the power of 'freewriting' as a writing technique:

> the theory is that writing and thinking go together, that is, you don't research and think and then write, you do both together: one enhances the other, or as E.M. Forster is reported to have said, 'How do I know what I think until I see what I say?' Or Joan Didion: 'I don't know what I think until I write it down'. (Katz, 2018: 61)

Freewriting is writing freely on your topic. Try writing from memory about the different ideas you have read and where they all fit together to support your argument. It might be that some of them now don't fit as well as you thought they did initially.

To help you to think about the topic you're focusing on for an assignment and what you would like to write about start to freewrite for 10 minutes. Starting with the reading you've done and the lecture and seminar notes you've compiled, write down the thoughts that you have about the topic. Once you've got the ideas on the page, can you make connections between the points, are there any pieces of literature you can draw on? Can you place the key authors and pieces of literature with particular points? It may be that it's a bit vague in places but that's fine at this stage in the writing process, or even a good thing because it's identified an area where you may need to do a bit more thinking, or reading, or both. It may also be a confidence boost as you realize that you know more about the topic and understand the connections between ideas more than you thought you did!

ACTIVITY 3.3

Constructing an argument

Consider the question:

'Smartphones are having a negative impact on young people's education.' To what extent do you agree with this statement?
Consider: what are the possible responses to this question?

- Smartphones are having a negative impact on young people's education:

- Smartphones can increase young people's access to social media and cyber-bullying and this can have a negative effect on their sense of self. Young people spend more time on their device than learning. The devices are a distraction.

- Smartphones are having a positive impact on young people's education:
  - Devices can be used to support higher-level thinking in the classroom e.g. research and digital tasks.

- Smartphones may* have a negative impact on *some* young people's education:
  - There are many perspectives to consider. It depends on the individual young person or group of young people.
  (* notice that we have said 'may have' here to signal hedging – please see section in Chapter 4 about the technique called hedging).

You should also consider the 'to what extent' aspect of this question as it is asking you to consider and comment on whether you agree with the statement or not. You might have come up with the following responses to this part of the question:

- Smartphones can have a negative impact on young people's education.
- Smartphones can have a positive impact on young people's education.

It depends on a variety of different factors including the young person and the educational context (for example digital literacy skills can improve with the use of smartphones).

> **TIP**
>
> Now that you have your argument-claim and counter argument-claim you can begin to draw on relevant literature and use it as evidence to support your points. Remember to ensure the academic sources are credible (see Chapter 2). With topics such as technology and social media, it can be tempting to draw on online resources. However, you need to check the authenticity and credibility of these. Academic, scholarly and peer-reviewed sources are more appropriate because they help to provide stronger evidence to support your arguments.

ACTIVITY 3.4

Developing critical thinking and credibility of argument(s) – a reminder

As we are looking at the educational issue of smartphone use in children and young people in the previous Activity Box 3.3 to consider to what extent we agree with the statement *'Smartphones are having a negative impact on young people's education'* take a look at the BBC InDepth piece (https://tinyurl.com/48h6bjyf) entitled 'The debate: Should smartphones be banned for under 16s' exploring whether Smartphones should be banned for children and young people under this age.

Read the conversational piece between Chris Vallance (a senior technology reporter), Daisy Greenwell (a co-founder of the campaign group Smartphone Free Childhood) and Sonia Livingstone (a Professor at LSE and leader of the university's research centre for children's digital rights).

- **Consider** what different pieces of evidence there are available to you:
    - What is the evidence?
    - Is it credible?
    - Can any of the sources be used to provide evidence for the responses (e.g smartphones are having a positive impact or a negative impact on young people's education or it depends on the wider context)?
    - Should you be cautious of a source like this?

Student response: Reading this debate presented in a conversational format between Chris Vallance, Daisy Greenwell and Sonia Livingstone does provide some areas which could be explored as a starting point to address the question: *'Smartphones are having a negative impact on young people's education.' To what extent do you agree with this statement?*

However, we need to be cautious of using this media source. We need to be cautious of any media/web-based sources we use because they may not be authentic or reliable. Instead, we can research the two speakers and whether they have conducted any research, or written any peer-reviewed publications about the topic.

remember to keep an open mind when constructing an argument. It's important to be flexible and open to the possibility of having to change the direction of the argument, depending on the research. Also remember to answer the question or address the task brief. The work should not just state everything you know about the topic.

How to map out your argument

Once you have an idea of what you would like the focus of your work to be and what the argument is, an annotated plan with the key bibliographic information can help to visualize the argument. It provides a space to suggest what relevant literature will be included and to make notes on how each of the sources contributes to your developing argument. Here is a starter example using the content from the critical thinking grid.

Example:
Essay title/topic:

'Pupils in secondary schools should be educated in single-sex classrooms' – *To what extent do you agree with this statement? Please draw on relevant academic literature and related documents.*

Introduction

- This debate has received educational attention from educators, researchers and policy makers for decades (Harker, 2000; Younger and Warrington, 2002).
- Thesis statement – Disagree (but to what extent? Inconclusive literature).
- Signposting for the reader: 1. Will provide a brief historical overview; 2. Will discuss some key literature which suggests it depends on the context; 3. Finally will conclude.

Historical overview

- e.g. Younger and Warrington (2002).

Complex situation

- It's important to also focus on intersectionality (Harker, 2000; Kenway et al., 1998; Murphy and Elwood, 1998).
- What roles do social class and ethnicity play in addition to gender?

- Is this a moral panic? (e.g. Jewkes, 2004). Media hype about achievement, exam results and academic grades? In reality there may not be such significant gaps. (Clavel and Flannery, 2022).

Conclusion

- Is the agenda set by media in relation to exam results and achievement shaping public perceptions? What about STEM subjects?
- But there's an assumption the audience are passive recipients rather than constructing meaning.

Every student will have their own personal viewpoints about which type of plans are most accessible and useful to them. Although there is much heated debate in the Educational Research literature about whether learning styles exist or if they are a myth (see Li et al., 2016), every learner will have a preference for a particular approach to planning essay writing. See Barrow and Westrup (2019), Chapter 6, for more ideas on ways to plan your work.

Obstacles to analysing sources critically and how to overcome them

1 Time – a big one!

Reading tasks and bringing together all of your notes on the different sources always takes longer than you think. Yet, this is often a task where students can underestimate the amount of time required. Some students may work better under pressure, but try to give yourself some additional time to complete the task. It's very difficult to estimate how long it might take to complete a piece of assessment. You could help yourself here by noting down how many tasks you've done in a study session to help you with your planning in the future. For example, in a two-hour session, perhaps you skim-read one chapter, and read another in depth and made notes? Then consider roughly how many sources you might need for one assessment, and calculate an indication of how many days you might need to put aside to undertake the reading and research (remembering that this is the work required even before any writing takes place! Another reason as to why assignments simply can't be left until the last minute). It's a good idea to have an idea of the time you'll need and then add another hour for each study session! If you don't need to use the time for study, you have some bonus time!

2 Finding the sources
Once you have roughly planned the time it's going to take to do the reading and bring all your notes together (and added a bit of extra time) you need to find the sources you're going to use. The majority of these will be journal articles and books – academic peer-reviewed sources. Depending on the assessment, you may also be required to find legislation and policy documents. Your university library webpages will be able to help guide you to access these different resources. If you use AI to help you find any sources, make sure you fact check them against your own knowledge and understanding and sources that you know are academic and peer-reviewed. Remember the AI output can be incorrect, biased and or misleading.

3 Who am I to say?
There are times when you may feel unsure about a topic you're studying, your understanding of it and perhaps just generally less confident with your studies. This is completely normal and something that most people will experience (whether they're comfortable to admit it to others, or not). However, if you find yourself experiencing these types of feelings for the majority of the time with your studies, you may be experiencing 'Imposter Syndrome'. As Holden et al. (2024: 726) highlight, students may also 'fear being found out to be a fraud' and have less confidence in their own voice and level to feel sufficiently informed to critically think about the literature and present their argument(s). If you find yourself questioning your own voice and whether you can write or say particular points, remind yourself that you can put into place the strategies and approaches we are recommending in this book and keep coming back to the idea that you are being an organized, systematic, critical thinker who has every right to express their (well-informed!) voice and viewpoint. For example, you can use the 'freewriting' activity introduced earlier in this chapter to try to remember what you know about the topic. You may remember more than you think and this could be a confidence boost. Once you have identified the key ideas, concepts and any important readings, try to make connections between the points. Can you identify similarities and differences or viewpoints and opposing views? You could also use AI as a tutor to check your ideas and understanding. However, it's important to complete the other activities and develop your own voice first so that you're using AI as a resource to confirm your ideas

rather than before to generate them. It's important that it is your voice in your work and not AI – you do not need to rely on AI.

4 Our bias

In Chapter 2 we looked at a range of biases. Our own biases – particular beliefs and perspectives we have about concepts and everyday situations, based on our own thoughts and experiences – can have an impact on our critical thinking. For example, if one of your class peers always arrives to the morning lecture 20 minutes late, you may think that they are lazy and disorganized. However, it could be because they have a morning schedule which requires them to care for a relative, or to drop children off at school, or the transport links and timetables could make getting to a lecture for 9am impossible. If you prioritize your bias you will miss important information and make claims, assumptions and connections that are not true.

With critical thinking, and to engage with the process effectively, it is important that we can recognize our own biases. Take a look back at Chapter 2 to remind yourself of the different types of bias and strategies to help with these.

5 Getting into the habit of critical analysis

Be critical throughout the year, not just at assessment time! It's good practice to get into the habit of recording your thoughts and ideas about your reading throughout the academic year, not just when you're studying and focusing on an assignment. Some students use an electronic format such as an Excel spreadsheet whereas others prefer to write in a notebook, or you might capture them in a notes or audio section of your phone so that you always have them with you. You know what works best for you in your studies. It is important that there is space within the note-keeping tool for you to expand the list of authors and research. Keeping track of the topic area, the authors and research focus will enable you to come to know who the main authors are and what they are writing about. For example, you could use descriptive headings that refer to the module or unit the notes are relevant to, and key ideas or theories that are featured. However, remember to keep an open mind and to also read about the work of other less well-known authors in the research area. Take a moment to think about the referencing information and whether there are any social relations excluded from the discussion e.g. gender, ethnicity, disability, culture, social class and so on. Can you find more representative literature?

To get into a critical mindset, being critical about the information presented to you and that which you consume outside of your studies will also help you to think critically on your course. For example, the ways in which you consume information about current affairs or documentaries presented on the television or through podcasts or the decisions you make when buying an expensive new item.

> **ACTIVITY 3.5**
>
> **Making decisions**
>
> Think about a time when you had to make an important purchase. How did you weigh up the decision about what to buy – and where to buy it?

> **TIPS**
>
> To develop your critical thinking every day inside and outside of your course:
>
> - Try to keep up to date with educational issues in the news, developments, debates and policies so that you can draw on examples from the 'real world';
> - Think about your own experiences when you're reading an article for a seminar and ask yourself questions about whether your experiences, or those of your friends and siblings, were similar or different;
> - Don't just accept what you read as true, or the only way to look at something. This is true for the media and academic sources. Always try to consider at least one other point of view – I try to think of two so that I can then compare;
> - When taking notes in lectures make a note of the key points given by the lecturer, and also use a different coloured pen, or if typing a different font to ask your own questions – I find this helps to keep critically active;
> - When reading seminar readings in advance of sessions, ask a question on each paragraph so that you can go and explore this in the seminar with peers. The questions can be related to the content of the text, style and format or methodology if it's an article about a research study.

6 Thinking critically together with other students

Thinking critically together with other students can support your critical thinking and analysis. Studying Education and Childhood Studies related degrees, it's likely that you will be required to work together with other students in a group. This could be working together on tasks in class, formative assessments and possibly summative assessments. It's a good idea to get into the habit of being able to work with others in a group and think critically, productively and successfully. Building habits like this can take time so it's best to start early in your degree. You will also develop key skills and capabilities for employability as you develop through working in a group and thinking critically (read more around these skills for employability in Chapter 7).

To be a valuable group member and critical thinker, you also need to understand more about yourself and working in a group. Ask yourself these questions:

- How will I work in a group?
- What roles am I good at?
- What roles can I develop if given the opportunity?
- What contributions can I make?
- How can I support others?

ACTIVITY 3.6

Reflection

Think about a time when you worked as part of a group and consider the following questions:

- What roles did you have when working in the group?
- Do you feel you work well in a group? What are your strengths?
- Are there any areas of group-working you can develop?
- Do you have any reservations about working in a group? What are they? Can you identify any ways to reduce or remove them?

TIPS

Successful group work

What does successful group work look like?

Designated roles, everyone supports each other, communication, even better – good communication, equal workload and effort, everyone working together.

Some 'ground rules' for working together to be successful:

- Make sure everyone knows that they should contribute equally;
- Respect everybody's opinions so people feel they can contribute;
- Actively listen to each other's points of view and include everyone.

It's important to be flexible and have the flexibility to adopt different perspectives. It's not about looking for the *right* answer, but more about learning to develop our knowledge and understanding.

What to do if or when you're feeling overwhelmed

Feeling overwhelmed and anxious can have a limiting impact on our ability to be a critical thinker. It can make any of the obstacles listed above more prominent which makes the process of critical thinking and being a critical thinker harder. Here are some tips:

- Take a break – with so much information available, sometimes making a start can feel daunting. If you feel like this, take a break and put some distance between yourself and the information or the work you're completing. Putting this distance between yourself and the task will mean that you can come back to it with a fresh perspective.
- Talk it through – as Neil Mercer (2000: 98) states 'reasoning is more visible in the talk'. Talking your ideas through with your peers or lecturers can help you to make the links and support your critical thinking. Maybe even just verbalizing your thoughts out loud to yourself (or recording and listening back to them) can be helpful to 'hear' arguments.
- Freewriting – in a similar way to talking through the critical thinking ideas, free-flow writing, where you just write continuously for a set time e.g. five minutes can help you to free up the ideas. No need to worry about anyone reading it, it's just for you, and your own understanding.

Summing up

Once you have started to read and analyse sources (we're seeing 'read' in the widest possible way and not just referring to written text but a range of sources including documentaries and podcasts for example, as well as the written text), it's important to have an organization system that works for you. This can include a system for organizing the critical thinking about the sources that have been analysed and the bibliographic information. This will help you to draw all of the information together in an accessible way so that you can plan for your assignments.

Working with sources requires an element of criticality in order to identify and analyse arguments you discover as you engage with varied ideas and perspectives. Developing practices to help you feel more confident in your approach to sources will help you to become not only a more critical learner, but a more effective one, too.

References

Barrow, C. and Westrup. R. (2019), *Writing Skills for Education Students*, London: Red Globe Press.

Birrell Ivory, S. (2021), *Becoming a Critical Thinker: For your University Studies and Beyond*, Oxford: Oxford University Press.

Clavel, J.G. and Flannery, D. (2022), 'Single-sex Schooling, Gender and Educational Performance: Evidence Using PISA Data', *British Educational Research Journal*, 49: 248–65.

Harker, R. (2000), 'Achievement, Gender and the Single-Sex/Coed Debate', *British Journal of Sociology of Education*, 21 (2): 203–18.

Holden, C.L., Wright, L., Herring, A. and Sims, P. (2024), 'Imposter Syndrome Among First- and Continuing-Generation College Students: The Roles of Perfectionism and Stress', *Journal of College Student Retention Research Theory and Practice*, 25 (3): 726–40.

Jewkes, Y. (2004), *Media & Crime: Key Approaches to Criminology*, London: SAGE Publications.

Katz, L. (2018), *Critical Thinking and Persuasive Writing for Postgraduates*, London: Palgrave Macmillan.

Kenway, J., Willis, S., Blackmore, J. and Rennie, L. (1998), *Answering Back: Girls, Boys and Feminism in Schools*, London: Routledge.

Li, Y., Medwell, J., Wray, D., Wang, L and Liu, X. (2016), 'Learning Styles: A Review of Validity and Usefulness', *Journal of Education and Training Studies*, 4 (10): 90–94.

Mercer, N. (2000), *Words and Minds: How We Use Language to Think Together*, London: Routledge.

Murphy, P. and Elwood, J. (1998), 'Gendered Learning Outside and Inside School: Influences on Achievement', in D. Epstein, J. Elwood, V. Hey and J. Maw (eds), *Failing Boys? Issues in Gender and Achievement*, 162–82, Buckingham: Open University Press.

Younger, M. and Warrington, M. (1996), 'Differential Achievement of Boys and Girls at GCSE: Some Observations from the Perspective of One School', *British Journal of Sociology of Education*, 17: 299–313.

Younger, M. and Warrington, M. (2002), 'Single-sex Teaching in a Co-educational Comprehensive School in England: An Evaluation Based Upon Students' Performance and Classroom Interactions', *British Educational Research Journal*, 28 (3): 353–74.

CHAPTER 4

How to Write Critically (and Evidence This)

At university, students are required to write academically,[1] and a key part of this writing process is to evidence critical thinking and analysis. Depending on how long you have been at university and how much academic writing you have done, you may have heard your lecturers and tutors say phrases like 'you need to be more critical' and 'can you question the findings more?' or received written comments such as 'more evidence needed' and 'this is descriptive rather than analytical'. In Chapters 2 and 3 we have looked at how you can read critically (and widely) and how to analyse sources individually and together (synthesis). In academic work the idea is that thinking and writing go together (Katz, 2018). In this chapter we will focus on:

- how your critical reading and critical thinking about educational issues and concepts and the evidence you have collected can be presented in critical writing.

What does critical writing look like?

> **TIP**
>
> Many of the **emboldened** words we use throughout the book are defined and expanded upon in the Glossary, at the end. Keep checking in with this and add your own annotations and further understandings.

Critical writing draws on relevant and appropriate sources as evidence to show the wider context being discussed and that your work is more than just your **subjective opinion**. A subjective opinion is when an idea or statement is presented but there is no evidence provided to support this. In critical writing you are providing more than just your opinion, you're

57

developing an **argument** based on the evidence. So, an **argument** is a claim that is presented and supported with examples and evidence. Your lecturers may use different words when they talk about arguments. For example, they may also refer to a 'claim' or 'main focus' when talking about an argument. **The argument is your response to the question or task that you have been given to answer.**

As part of the argument, there is also an **evaluation** and **interrogation** of the **evidence** provided. This requires you to assess the quality of the source you're using to provide the evidence and to question it: you should not just take the source as given and at face value.

Critical writing is also **well-balanced**. The topic of the critical writing is addressed from different viewpoints with arguments and counter-arguments. Due to word limits on assignments, it's not expected that all viewpoints will be covered in an assignment, but you need to demonstrate knowledge and understanding of more perspectives than just the main one being presented.

It's important to not be too critical or negative in your critical writing. Often the words 'critical' or 'critique' are associated with being negative or finding fault with an idea or concept. This isn't the case. Being critical does not always mean having to critique an idea, concept or piece of literature in a negative way. Instead, it is possible to critically appraise and engage with critical thinking and writing in a positive way. It depends on the content, the context and the arguments being presented.

When writing critically, unless you are required to, for example in a reflective assignment, you should avoid making **assertions** or **assumptions** based on thoughts and experiences, rather than the evidence. Try to avoid sentences like 'I think …' or 'in my opinion …'. By drawing on sources and literature you are providing evidence which supports your arguments and this support transforms your writing from an opinion or thought to an argument.

How do you present critical thinking in your writing?

After you have spent many hours researching, reading, making notes, thinking critically about a topic, making more notes and doing more reading and critical thinking, you will be ready to begin to construct an argument.

How to Write Critically (and Evidence This) 59

Embedding these components in your own writing – constructing an argument, logical reasoning, sequencing, premise and credibility – will strengthen the criticality and go towards ensuring the individuality and authenticity of your work. Constructing arguments involves synthesizing all the critical reading and research and critical thinking. **Synthesizing means putting together different parts to make a new whole.** For example, a synthesis of the literature brings together the reviews and notes made on the different readings of the literature. In Chapter 3 we looked at how you organize your sources and notes of critical reading and thinking to evidence, support and construct an argument and now we're going to focus on how this is presented in academic writing and how you can demonstrate your own critical voice.

Structuring your academic paragraphs (constructing, linking and signposting)

Look carefully at journal articles you come across in your reading. Do you notice any patterns when it comes to the structuring of the paragraphs? Within academic texts there are often noticeable patterns in the ways they are constructed or written. Generally, you may notice that the paragraphs have the following structure which uses the **'PEEL'** acronym (see Figure 4.1):

- **Point/topic sentence** – the paragraph begins with a topic sentence, telling the reader about the focus and purpose of the paragraph. It can also give the reader an indication of your voice and the perspective being presented;
- **Explanation** – these sentences support the direction of the topic sentence;
- **Evidence/examples** – these sentences provide evidence and/or examples from the literature to help to illustrate the point;
- **Link** – this final sentence links to the next point. Remind the reader of the argument and the direction of this.

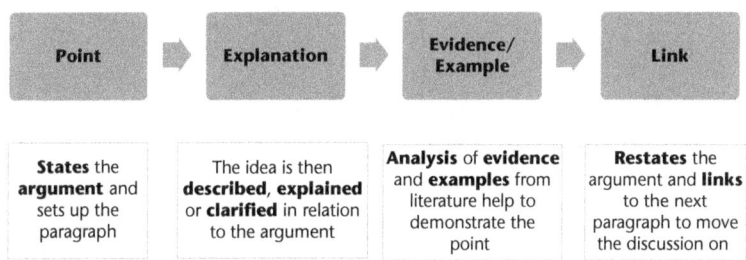

Figure 4.1 Point, Explanation, Evidence, Link

> **An example of using the PEEL structure**
>
> This paragraph provides the introduction to an assignment which is responding to the following assignment brief:
>
> *Identify an area of specific Special Educational Needs and Disability (SEND) and critically consider any educational needs.*
>
> The student has decided to focus on pupils with chronic health conditions, especially inflammatory bowel disease (IBD), and their educational needs.
>
> **Point/topic sentence:** Inclusive education has been identified as a significant issue in government legislation and current practices (Hodkinson, 2023), yet more support is needed for pupils with special educational needs and disability (SEND) and in particular chronic health conditions.
>
> **Explanation:** Since the introduction of the Warnock Report (1978) there has been increasing research focusing on the educational experiences of pupils with SEND and making the UK education system more inclusive for all learners. There has been an increasing emphasis on the social model of disability (Hodkinson, 2023).
>
> **Evidence/example:** This model of disability places the pupils at the heart of the education system and is critical of the ways in which society and the learning environment can create barriers (Nutbrown and Clough, 2013). SEND legislation such as the SEND Code of Practice (Department for Education, 2014) has been the mechanism for changes to policy and practice and it is significant to note that chronic health conditions were included in the revised 2014 documentation. Despite this emphasis on inclusion to include pupils with chronic health conditions, the needs of pupils with inflammatory bowel disease (IBD) such as Crohn's Disease and Ulcerative Colitis have been overlooked (Freckmann et al., 2018).
>
> **Link:** Focusing on the educational needs of pupils with IBD, this essay will explore learning needs and identify potential barriers ...

How do you incorporate evidence effectively in your writing to support criticality?

Earlier in the book we have looked at what makes arguments credible. Using evidence effectively will help you to do this and demonstrate your critical thinking. Three ways you can do this are by using direct

How to Write Critically (and Evidence This)   61

quotations, paraphrasing and summarizing the work of others from the relevant literature. Here are some of the differences between them:

1. **Direct quotations** where you reproduce someone else's words precisely, word for word and acknowledge this. Direct quotations are considered a good idea when:
   - The quotation includes some important terminology;
   - You feel that you want to convey the exact same words because the author has expressed the viewpoint in such a well-expressed and relevant way;
   - You can use the quotation to support your viewpoints and build on the argument(s) being made.

ACTIVITY 4.1

Finding a logical flow

Put the sentences into a logical structure. Think about the reasoning, sequencing and the language used to present the sentences in a logical and coherent paragraph.

Sentences	Order in paragraph (e.g. point/ topic sentence = 1)
Looking at primary school data they highlight how girls outperform boys in every subject, with a notable difference in reading and writing. This is concerning as supporting boys with English, reading and writing have been the focus of educationalists and policy-makers for over 20 years (see for example Younger et al., 2005) and the issues still remain.	
Previously, interventions such as those detailed by Younger et al. have focused on the inside of the classroom – pedagogical group and individual approaches, structural approaches e.g. comparing single-sex and co-educational classes and socio-cultural approaches, particularly between school and home contexts.	

Sentences	Order in paragraph (e.g. point/ topic sentence = 1)
One strategy that could be used in the classroom and home-school partnership is active reading socialization (van Hek and Kraaykamp, 2023).	
van Hek and Kraaykamp (2023) for example investigated why boys are less intrinsically motivated to read than girls. Santa Maria et al. (2022) have explored the role of digital media and the impact it has on reading motivation and reading engagement in a systematic review.	
There is a gender achievement gap between male and female students at every level of education, with female students outperforming male students in examination results and progression into tertiary education (Cavaglia et al., 2021).	
Cavaglia et al. (2021) look at how the achievement gap in England has developed since 2000.	
More recently studies have focused on links between home and school reading socialization and intrinsic reading motivation of girls and boys.	
They highlight how important it is for children and young people 'to feel what they read and enact it. In other words, make it their own' (Santa Maria et al., 2022: 13). They suggest that schools must facilitate and support their students with this.	
However, it should be noted that students' preferences for how to achieve this will vary so it is important the educators consider students' voices in this process to continue to develop this area.	

Some students who are at the beginning of their studies and academic educational journey say that it feels 'safer' to use direct quotations as they are still learning and developing their knowledge and understanding of educational theories and research. However, when students use direct quotations, they do not really demonstrate criticality in their writing, just that they can copy a relevant quotation. They can also take up a significant amount of word count so think about whether direct quotes are the most appropriate source to support your argument and demonstrate criticality. If you do decide to include direct quotes, you also need to show why you have used it and why it is meaningful (but don't fall into the trap of presenting a quote and then simply re-writing it in your own words afterwards). When using a direct quotation: make sure you copy the quote exactly, and keep any original emphasis used by the author (e.g. using italics); use quotation marks, include the details of the author(s), date of publication and page number and use text to embed and introduce the quotation, for example:

As Davies and Barnett (2015: 9) state, 'critical thinking, as both skills and dispositions, is mainly about the development of the *individual*' (original emphasis).

2 **Paraphrasing** the work of others' writing, ideas, arguments and the ways they have used or referred to educational concepts, when selecting relevant literature as evidence can help you to demonstrate critical thinking in your work. Paraphrasing is when you use the work of others by acknowledging the author and/or the source, summarize it and rephrase their ideas in your own words. As we said in our earlier book, Barrow and Westrup (2019: 28), '*a paraphrase is your own interpretation and expression of ideas expressed by someone else*' (original emphasis).

3 **Summarizing** the work of others' writing, ideas, arguments and the ways they have used or referred to educational concepts can be helpful to demonstrate your understanding. You may be asked to summarize a research article for example. To summarize, try to use the fewest words to write – in your own words – what the text is about and what it is telling you.

When you paraphrase or summarize the work of others in your writing, you need to reference it using the appropriate in-text citation and full bibliographic information in the reference list.

> **Paraphrasing and summarizing**
>
> Here is an example of how you can paraphrase a direct quote.
>
> **Direct quote and original text:** 'if sufficient skills are to be in place to meet the needs of the green transition, it is essential that strategically important jobs linked to the fight against climate change are well signalled to young people and that they are helped in their understanding of, and progression towards them' (Chang and Mann, 2024: 6).
>
> **Paraphrase example:** The author reminds us that it is important that young people are equipped with the skills and knowledge required to help them to understand the increasing shift towards green careers and that young people can access jobs linked to these (Chang and Mann, 2024: 6).
>
> **Summarize example:** To summarize Chang and Mann (2024: 6), it's important to help young people to know what green jobs that support positive climate change are available and what skills are required.
>
> **Note:** When you paraphrase and summarize, you must still include the reference to acknowledge where you have taken the idea or information from.

When you paraphrase and summarize the literature, you are required to take the original text and write the points in your own words. Your wording is also often shorter in length than the original. This means that you can demonstrate that you understand the ideas presented in the original text and express them in your own words. **Using paraphrasing or summarizing in your writing demonstrates understanding more than using direct quotations.** You can think and write critically about the literature you have read, and draw on more than one text. This helps to build the criticality as you're drawing on a few sources – and perspectives – to strengthen the point being made. As the evidence is embedded within your own writing, the text continues to flow and this also helps you to demonstrate your own academic voice. You must make sure that you remember to cite the author of the work you're paraphrasing as you go along, so that the source(s) of your ideas are clear.

To help you to paraphrase and summarize:

- Read the text you intend to paraphrase. You will probably need to do this more than once. As you are reading, write notes and ask yourself questions using some of the strategies we identified in Chapter 2. This

will help you to read the text in an active way to identify the key points and ensure you understand the main ideas.
- Put the text to one side so that you are not tempted to have a look at it again at the moment.
- Write your paragraph and paraphrase the original text.
- Re-read the text you have paraphrased to make sure you have written about the author's main arguments or idea. Double check that you have not included any direct quotations from the text. If you have, these will need appropriate citation.
- Remember to include the in-text citation in the main body of your writing and bibliographic information at the end in the reference list.

The following is an example of bad paraphrasing. This is considered a form of plagiarism. For more information about how to paraphrase in detail and understanding plagiarism, please see Barrow and Westrup (2019). Students should also ask their lecturers and seminar tutors or consult relevant university policies if they have any questions about their institutional plagiarism policies.

An example of bad paraphrasing

The original text is from Nyström, A.-S., Jackson, C. and Salminen Karlsson, M. (2018), 'What Counts as Success? Constructions of Achievement in Prestigious Higher Education Programmes', *Research Papers in Education*, 34 (4): 465–82.

Here is the original text from Nyström et al. (2018: 467):

'Like Jenkins (2004: 75), we see identity as a relational "trajectory of being and becoming", and a cumulative process of embodied, interactional accomplishments. A student's self-image, ability-beliefs and sense of belonging within the particular institution and programme can be seen as a trajectory which is directed by, inter alia, her/his participation in teaching–learning activities, interaction with peers, the identities peers ascribe to them and discourses about success. Lecturers' assessments of students' educational abilities are also important in this process. In professional programmes students are also involved in a process of developing a professional identity, including particular competences and attitudes. As Costello (2005: 23) suggests '[a] certified professional school graduate who cannot "walk the walk and talk the talk" will not seem like a true professional to others and will not be successful'. Through encounters with others, students learn what it means to be and become, for example, a law student and lawyer. Also, they come to understand the extent to which they fulfil or deviate from the required standards, and experience belonging or disconnection from the 'law community' (Costello, 2005). Like Burke (2006: 731) we argue that 'aspirations are not constructed exclusively at the individual level but are tied in with complex structural, cultural and discursive relations and practices'. Hence, we also consider ways in which the programmes' structural, cultural and professional differences relate to constructions of success, as well as other social category differences, most notably gender.'

Take a look at the following text which a student has presented in their assignment. Identify the examples of bad paraphrasing with us as we note them in a different font, bold and underlined.

Identity is a relational trajectory of being and becoming (Jenkins, 2004). **There is no signalling of the direct quotation and the authors (Nyström et al., 2018) who have cited Jenkins are not mentioned.** From my experience, my student self-image, ability-beliefs and sense of belonging within the university have been linked to teaching–learning activities, interaction with my peers, the identities peers ascribe to me and our stories of success. **Text has been changed to fit with the student's perspective as they reflect on their experience and some words have been changed e.g. the word 'discourse' has been changed to 'stories' but this is not enough and the original authors of the text should be cited.** In professional programmes students are also involved in a process of developing a professional identity, including particular competences and attitudes. As Costello (2005: 23) suggests '[a] certified professional school graduate who cannot "walk the walk and talk the talk" will not seem like a true professional to others and will not be successful'. **The citation is correct, but the student should have clearly cited that this quotation was in Nyström et al. (2018) and this is where they have taken it from.** Through being with other students, students learn what it means to be and become, for example, a law student and lawyer or an education student and an educator e.g. teacher. **Here the student has added an example related to their degree and professional practice without acknowledging the original text.**

Writing introductions and conclusions

As we discussed in the *Writing Skills for Education Students* book (Barrow and Westrup, 2019), introductions and conclusions are crucial to assignments. Introductions provide a context for the assignment and 'signposting' in terms of what you're going to do in the assignment and how you're going to achieve this. The 'signposting' provides signs and directions for your reader to follow. Within the introduction you can also explain and/or define or 'unpack' any key terms of concepts that may be central to the work.

Consider the following steps adapted from Barrow and Westrup (2019: 64) to help you to draft an introduction:

- What is or what are the key issues that the work is concerned with?
- Why is this or are these important?
- Why is the issue, or why are the issues worthy of exploration?
- What key sections or discussions will it therefore be necessary to cover?
- Provide signposting for the reader. What can the reader expect and how will you ensure this is covered? Tell them.

The conclusion is equally important to the assignment. It provides a summary of the points covered, highlights clearly how the work has addressed the task brief, gives an indication of why the topic matters (and the significance of this) and offers up a judgement on the issues under consideration.

An effective conclusion should:

- Make it clear how the work has 'answered' the essay question or 'responded' well to the assignment brief and task set.
- Present some kind of judgement or concluding ideas (even if these remain somewhat neutral rather than a definitive yes/no response).

Try to synthesize the many details you have put into the work into a few broader, overall points (Barrow and Westrup, 2019: 67).

Please see Barrow and Westrup (2019) for further details and examples.

How do you find your own voice and demonstrate criticality?

When you are writing academically, it is important to present your critical thinking and analysis with your own voice. This helps to provide authenticity in your work.

Finding, and then presenting your own voice in academic writing is a skill that can develop with practice, although care is needed in order to achieve this. Below are some ways you can find your own voice.

The way you introduce the evidence

The way you draw on relevant literature as evidence can help you to present your critical voice. Your voice will be stronger if you introduce the author at the beginning of the sentence and use words to show that you understand the impact of the author, their research findings or policy documentation and so on. In Activity 4.1 we looked at paraphrasing a direct quote. We can continue to develop the paraphrase example to add more of your own voice to the text:

> Chang and Mann (2024: 6) state that it is important that young people are equipped with the skills and knowledge required to help them to understand the increasing shift towards green careers and that young people can access jobs linked to these.

By moving the in-text citation and the authors' names to the beginning of the sentence, the voice is stronger. It signals a confidence to the reader that this writer has done their reading and can present the information. The writer is not 'hiding' behind the direct quotation or the authors as with the direct quote and first paraphrase example.

Using 'hedging' language

Using hedging language means writing in **a more cautious way** to avoid a strong tone, overgeneralizations and the writing coming across to the reader as biased. When writers adopt this strategy, they're showing that they understand there are the ideas from this one perspective, and that there could also be a variety of perspectives and other ideas to consider too. After all, it's not possible to cover every idea in an essay or assignment. The amount of hedging language used needs to be balanced though because too much hedging could indicate a lack of confidence in the ideas and or the conviction in the writing.

Examples of 'hedging' words and phrases from Academic Phrasebank[2]:

It may be ...
It could be ...
It might be ...
It suggests ...
It is likely ...

Avoid using the phrases 'I believe' and 'in my opinion' when presenting your argument (unless you have been specifically asked to do this). In academic writing you're demonstrating your criticality and drawing on evidence so what you're presenting is more than your 'beliefs' or 'opinions' – your writing is evidence-informed arguments.

> **TIP**
>
> When you are next drafting a piece of work and reviewing it, take a look at the sentences and consider how you could rewrite a sentence to include more hedging. What do you notice about the academic tone and your voice?

Know your audience

It is important to think about your audience and know who you are writing for. The audience may have differing knowledge about the topic you are writing about. In your writing for assessment purposes, make sure you are clear from your lecturers and tutors about the audience and level of knowledge required. An assessment may require you to focus on a specific audience e.g. pupils, peers, parents, teachers or policy-makers, so you may need to adjust your critical approach to meet their needs. For example, it's important to critically explain information from literature sources in different ways for children and adults. Demonstrating knowledge and understanding of a topic area are often criteria for assignments, so if you're not sure, double check with them.

What can you do to help find your critical voice?

Moving from the tasks of reading, thinking critically and making notes about topics, to writing about them academically requires a shift and consolidation in your identity as a writer. Sometimes students (and your lecturers) will question what this identity is, or looks like, and find that they lack confidence in writing and presenting their ideas and arguments. When this happens, they could be experiencing 'Imposter Syndrome'. Students often question 'who am I to say this?'.

Imposter Syndrome

As we mentioned briefly in the previous chapter, 'Imposter Syndrome' is becoming a much more well-known phenomenon which helps us to explain some of our uncertain feelings around expressing our own voice. It was first noted in 1978 by psychologists Pauline Clance and Suzanne Imes. It is the view shared by some people that they're not very intelligent and they 'have fooled anyone who thinks otherwise' (Clance and Imes, 1978: 241). Writing more recently, Wilkinson (2020: 364) outlines that 'imposter syndrome suggests that you believe your success was down to luck and your lack of ability will be exposed'. Within universities, undergraduate and postgraduate students, as well as their lecturers, can sometimes be affected by this lack of belief in their own abilities and it can have an impact on their writing, and sometimes overall engagement. If your writing is affected by imposter syndrome, try some of the tips below and speak with your university tutors or lecturers.

> **TIPS**
>
> **Top tips for dealing with imposter syndrome**
>
> If you experience imposter syndrome you may find the following helpful:
> - Acknowledge how you are feeling;
> - Keep a record of all of your achievements and things that make you feel good (this doesn't have to be academic). You can look back at this when you're experiencing these feelings to remind yourself about what you can do;
> - Talk to others – your peers may be experiencing similar feelings to a writing task so talk about it. Your lecturers or student support staff may have experienced it and be willing to share their suggestions with you;
> - Keep reading and learning – this will help you in developing and growing. You may just need to read something, or give yourself time for 'something to click' with your argument development;
> - And ultimately, remember that writing can be challenging and to give yourself regular breaks.

Writing critically, confidently

With critical thinking and academic writing, some students question whether they can really question the arguments and findings of expert authors in their work. Do you find yourself asking 'who am I to critique the work of key authors and experts?' and replying to yourself with 'I'm just a student!' like our students? Well, the answer is 'yes!', students can question the work, for example the findings and arguments, presented by key authors and experts in the area of Education Studies and related subjects. Here are some reasons why:

1 When you're studying for an Education degree (and related degrees e.g. Childhood and Youth) and thinking critically, there are no right or wrong answers. Instead, you're focusing on the arguments presented by others, comparing and contrasting these with each other and thinking critically about whether they are pieces of information you can trust.
2 Being critical doesn't mean critiquing others' work in a negative way and finding fault with it. You can also be critical of work in a positive way – highlighting the strengths and critically appraising the work.

3 We learn by asking, thinking about, and responding to the questions people raise – critically analysing articles and raising questions about the theories, methodologies and findings presented in them helps everyone to learn and develop their knowledge and understanding – including the authors and experts in the field.
4 You can link your ideas and arguments to practice which means that you can write with purpose. If you have work or placement experience that is relevant to an assignment, consider whether you can draw on this (see more of this in Chapter 7). You may be able to draw on the practical experience and contextualize this with relevant literature, or your experiences may motivate you to write passionately about educational policy implementation. It may not be appropriate to include your anecdotes in all assignments so check with your lecturer/tutor.

Questions to reflect upon in relation to writing

If you are experiencing difficulties with writing, ask yourself the following questions:

- What's your biggest challenge to writing?
- What do you do before you write?
- What do you do while writing?
- What do you do after writing?
- What's happening when your writing is going well?
- How could your approach be even better?

Try to keep a regular journal either using a notebook and pen or an online document to keep track of your thoughts, challenges and progress. Can you spot any patterns in terms of how you're approaching writing and what you're doing?

Productivity tips

Everyone has different productivity levels at different points in the academic year. Try these tips if you experience a dip in motivation and/or productivity. Or, you could establish these tips at the beginning of the academic year so that they become part of your studying routine.

Critical friend writing groups

As we mentioned in the previous section to help you to develop your confidence in critical thinking and writing, being critical doesn't always mean approaching someone's work in a negative way and criticizing it. Critical friend writing groups are a way that students can support each other in their writing. This can help if your motivation is disappearing as you need to 'show up' for your peers to support them, and them to support you. Find a peer or friend on your course who you trust and whose opinion you value, plan study and writing sessions together and review each other's work. Remember to be mindful of the university's policies on plagiarism and collusion where you're studying: writing together alongside one another does not mean writing the same thing.

> **TIPS**
>
> ### How to offer good support to peers
>
> - Meet regularly before (and/or after) your seminars and lectures to go through the key ideas from the lecture learning materials and seminar readings. This will help you to find peers that you 'click' with.
> - You don't necessarily have to agree with each other's viewpoints. What is important is that you feel able to talk and discuss the ideas, and that there is a mutual trust within the peer group.
> - Make sure you can attend the critical friend groups regularly, put the work in and reciprocate any tasks e.g. if your peer spends some time looking at a section of your work and gives you comments, make sure you can then do this for them when required.
> - Be honest and open with each other. Sometimes we have more commitments or busier weeks with appointments or events outside of the university, so we may need to plan around these.
> - Keep in regular contact. Do not just not show up for a group session.

ACTIVITY 4.2

My Approach to Writing

Reflect on your current approaches to writing and write these in the left column. Now spend a few minutes thinking about how you could make this approach better. We've reflected on our approaches to give you some examples.

My current approach	This could be even better if ....
I get distracted by my phone, so I silence notifications on my phone.	I placed the phone out of sight and reach.

My current approach	This could be even better if ....
I'm always anxious that I haven't done enough reading so I read, read and do more reading and then end up rushing before the deadline.	I plan in advance to ensure I looked at the reading list and give myself an approximate number of texts to read, covering the key ideas and read these weekly. I will then have enough information and can begin the assignment at least two weeks before the deadline.

What other aspects of your studies and approach to writing do you think you can improve? Try to think of ways to do this.

'Refresh' your writing through reading (more!)

Pat Thomas (2022) talks about 'refreshing' your writing through reading (more!) to remind yourself of what makes good writing. If you have access to exemplar portions of assignments similar to those you are working on this is always helpful to realign your expectations and what you're working towards. Thomas suggests:

> Read it slowly looking at the writing. What mood does the writer create? How does the writer manage the pace of their narrative? How do they use sentence structure and length to convey rhythm? If there is direct speech used, how is it introduced and incorporated? What metaphors are used? Are there novel categorisations? How did the writer manage their tenses? Where, how and why did they use adjectives and adverbs and to what effect? What kind of punctuation did they use?

What will help you to be able to confidently critique the work of key authors and experts is reading (more!) widely around the relevant topic areas. This will help you to develop your knowledge of key ideas, different perspectives, different theories and how others have applied them in other work. It will help you to think critically and support your arguments about why you agree or disagree with the author(s) you are reading, learning and writing about.

Remember to start researching and planning your assignments well in advance of the deadline. This will give you time to read, think critically about the topic and build the argument(s). You will have the time (and space) to go back to or read other literature if you wish to. Critical thinking cannot be hurried!

> Some students feel that they need to read and read and read and do not give themselves enough time to complete the writing of the assignment so it is rushed and last minute. Give yourself a 'pre-deadline' deadline to have completed the reading so that you give yourself time to think, draft, write, review, draft and write some more.

Editing writing and final checks

Once you have written your draft you will need to proofread and edit it before making any final checks. As we have suggested earlier in this chapter, it is important to give yourself plenty of time before the deadline to complete these tasks. Try these tips to support you with the editing process.

Thinking about your own (written) thinking

Being able to analyse your own writing is a key critical thinking skill. You need to be able to review your own writing and do this confidently. Some checklist questions to reflect on:

- ✓ What do you want the reader to take away?
- ✓ Are you clearly communicating your argument and critical thinking?
- ✓ Can you point to the evidence for the claim(s) you are making?
- ✓ How objective have you been with your presentation of the argument(s)? Are you willing to question your own views and are you open to the ideas of others?
- ✓ How did you decide to prioritize (include) some issues over others?
- ✓ Have you looked sufficiently for an opposing viewpoint? You need to be willing to reconsider your argument and possibly make changes to strengthen the writing e.g. to make the argument stronger.
- ✓ Are you confident in your own writing? E.g. have you really provided enough supporting evidence for your argument? (See the 'well, who says this?' test mentioned below).
- ✓ Is there any bias in your writing?
- ✓ What kinds of issues are still surrounded by uncertainty?
- ✓ How could you add more detail for precision?
- ✓ How could you rewrite a sentence to be more hedging?
- ✓ Might your 'answer' or 'response' have looked different ten years ago? If so, why?
- ✓ Is there an appropriate academic tone in your assignment?
- ✓ Is your spelling, punctuation and grammar correct?

Give yourself time in your planning, drafting and writing schedule

You need this time so that you can have some distance between yourself as a writer and yourself as an editor. You will need to look at the work as an editor and be objective. You will be more effective as an editor if you can give yourself some time and space so that you're not so familiar with the vocabulary and structure of the text.

The 'well, who says this?' test

This test will help you to see if further evidence or explanation is required. When you're reading your work from the position of an editor, if you find you can ask 'well, who said this?' you will need to provide further evidence from relevant literature. You may also need to unpack the idea a little further.

Read the work aloud and backwards, focusing on the words

First, read the work aloud. This will help you to focus on the words and the flow of your writing. Then, read the work backwards sentence by sentence, starting with the last word in the final sentence of the conclusion. Similarly to reading aloud, starting at this point and reading backwards will help you to focus on the words and the meaning of each sentence. Ask yourself – are they the correct words? Do they convey the expected meaning? Make every word count!

Summing up

This chapter explored how you can use critical thinking in your academic writing and ways to evidence this.

It has suggested ways to organize an assignment using the PEEL paragraph structure and variations of this to try to develop academic tone once you feel confident with the initial structure.

It has discussed the different ways of using literature and sources as evidence and the differences between directly quoting from sources, paraphrasing and summarizing. The discussion concluded that paraphrasing and summarizing help you to demonstrate understanding, and direct quotations should only be used if it refers to terminology or there is no better way to write the sentence.

It has outlined the writing process and how you can use your voice and the evidence to write critically and confidently.

Finally, it has provided hints and tips for being productive in your writing.

References

Barrow, C. and Westrup. R. (2019), *Writing Skills for Education Students*, London: Red Globe Press.

Birrell Ivory, S. (2021), *Becoming a Critical Thinker: For your University Studies and Beyond*, Oxford: Oxford University Press.

Cavaglia, C., Machin, S., McNally, S. and Ruiz-Valenzuela, J. (2021), 'Gender, Achievement, and Subject Choice in English Education', *Oxford Review of Economic Policy*, 36 (4): 816–35.

Chang, Y. and A. Mann (2024), 'Enhancing Green Career Guidance Systems for Sustainable Futures', *OECD Education Working Papers*, No. 318, OECD Publishing, Paris, https://doi-org.uea.idm.oclc.org/10.1787/e6ad2d9c-en (accessed 26 August 2024).

Clance, P.R., and Imes, S. A. (1978), 'The Imposter Phenomenon in High Achieving Women: Dynamics and Therapeutic Intervention', *Psychotherapy: Theory, Research & Practice*, 15 (3): 241–47. https://doi.org/10.1037/h0086006 (accessed 7 May 2025).

Davies, M. and Barnett, R. (2015), *The Palgrave Handbook of Critical Thinking in Higher Education*, Basingstoke: Palgrave Macmillan.

Department for Education (2014), *Special Educational Needs and Disabilities Code of Practice*. Available at: https://www.gov.uk/government/publications/send-code-of-practice-0-to-25 (accessed 9 November 2024).

Freckmann, M., Seipp, A., Laass, M.W., Koletzko, S., Claßen, M., Ballauff, A., Peplies, J. and Timmer, A. (2018), 'School-related Experience and Performance with Inflammatory Bowel Disease: Results from a Cross-Sectional Survey in 675 Children and their Parents', *BMJ Open Gastroenterology*, 5: 1–13.

Hodkinson, A. (2023), *Key Issues in Special Educational Needs, Disability and Inclusion*, London: SAGE Publications.

Katz, L. (2018), *Critical Thinking and Persuasive Writing for Postgraduates*, London: Palgrave Macmillan.

Nutbrown, C. and Clough, P. (2013), *Inclusion in the Early Years*, 2nd edition, London: SAGE Publications.

Nyström, A.-S., Jackson, C. and Salminen Karlsson, M. (2018), 'What Counts as Success? Constructions of Achievement in Prestigious Higher Education Programmes', *Research Papers in Education*, 34 (4): 465–82.

Santa Maria, L., Aliagas, C. and Rutten, K. (2022), 'Youth's Literacy Socialisation Practices Online: A Systematic Review of Research', *Learning, Culture and Social Interaction*, 34, 1–16.

Thomas, P. (2022), *Refresh your Writing Ideas*. Available at: https://tinyurl.com/mux79cwc (accessed 6 August 2024).

Vallance, C. (2024), BBC InDepth: The Debate: Should smartphones be banned for under 16s? Available at: https://www.bbc.co.uk/news/articles/cjd5z24d89vo (accessed 3 November 2024).

van Hek, M. and Kraaykamp, G. (2023), 'Why Jane Likes to Read and John Does Not: How Parents and Schools Stimulate Girls' and Boys' Intrinsic Reading Motivation', *Poetics*, 101.

Warnock, H.M. (1978), *Report of the Committee of Enquiry into the Education of Handicapped Children and Young People*. (HMSO Cmnd. 7212). Available at: https://webarchive.nationalarchives.gov.uk/ukgwa/20101007182820/http:/sen.ttrb.ac.uk/attachments/21739b8e-5245-4709-b433-c14b08365634.pdf (accessed 10 November 2024).

Wilkinson, C. (2020), 'Imposter Syndrome and the Accidental Academic: An Autoethnographical Account', *International Journal for Academic Development*, 25 (4): 363–74. https://doi.org/10.1080/1360144X.2020.1762087 (accessed 7 May 2025).

Younger, M. and Warrington, M. with Gray, J., Rudduck, J., McLellan, R., Bearne, E., Kershner, R. and Bricheno, P. (2005), *Raising Boys' Achievement*, London: DfES.

RESPONSE TO ACTIVITY 4.1

Finding the logical flow

There is a gender achievement gap between male and female students at every level of education, with female students outperforming male students in examination results and progression into tertiary education (Cavaglia et al., 2021). Cavaglia et al. (2021) look at how the achievement gap in England has developed since 2000. Looking at primary school data they highlight how girls outperform boys in every subject, with a notable difference in reading and writing. This is concerning as supporting boys with English, reading and writing have been the focus of educationalists and policy-makers for over 20 years (see for example Younger et al., 2005) and the issues still remain. Previously, interventions such as those detailed by Younger et al. have focused on the inside of the classroom – pedagogical group and individual approaches, structural approaches e.g. comparing single-sex and co-educational classes and socio-cultural approaches, particularly between school and home contexts. One strategy that could be used in the classroom and home-school partnership is active reading socialization (van Hek and Kraaykamp, 2023). More recently studies have focused on links between home and school reading socialization and intrinsic reading motivation girls' and boys'. Van Hek and Kraaykamp (2023) for example investigated why boys are less intrinsically motivated to read than girls. Santa Maria et al. (2022) have explored the role of digital media and the impact it has on reading motivation and reading engagement in a systematic review. They highlight how important it is for children and young people 'to feel what they read and enact it. In other words, make it their own' (Santa Maria et al., 2022: 13). They suggest that schools must facilitate and support their students with this. However, it should be noted that students' preferences for how to achieve this will vary so it is important the educators consider students' voices in this process to continue to develop this area.

Notes

1 For more detailed information about academic writing, please see Chapters 6–9 in our *Writing Skills for Education Students* book (Barrow and Westrup, 2019).

2 The University of Manchester has an excellent resource called the Academic Phrasebank (see https://www.phrasebank.manchester.ac.uk/). It has a wide range of phrases that you can use to help convey your intentions in academic work, such as how to introduce examples, present comparisons and explain causes and consequences. See also some of our helpful sentence starters and tips on language at the end of this book.

CHAPTER

5

How to Present Spoken Critical Thinking (and Evidence This)

In the previous chapters we've focused on how to think critically, developing an argument, critical voice and presenting critical thinking with written communication. In this chapter we will focus:

- on communicating critical thinking verbally, for example in seminars
- and visually in assessments such as presentations, podcasts and documentaries.

> **ACTIVITY 5.1**
>
> **Everyday talk?**
>
> Think about your day. How often do you use spoken word/speech to communicate? Is it with friends, family, university lecturers and peers, work colleagues? Does it vary in professional contexts, such as when you're at work, volunteering or undertaking a placement? What do you notice about the type of communication? For example, is it formal or informal? Is your language and tone different in different contexts?

Session talk: developing and presenting critical thinking in learning sessions

Engaging with verbal debates in lectures and seminars is one of the best ways you can try out and practise your critical thinking: good quality educational dialogue is linked to success (Heron, 2019). Drawing on the theory of socio-constructivist psychologist Vygotsky (1968), our talk and the discussions we have with others are key to developing thought.

Within classroom settings in schools, researchers such as Neil Mercer have illustrated the importance of 'exploratory talk', arguing that 'reasoning is more visible in the talk' (Mercer, 2000: 98). In a similar way, engaging in conversations in your university classrooms can help you to practise and rehearse your ideas and viewpoints, make connections, and encourage you to consider how you can support these; for example what literature you could draw on. Through discussions with your peers, you can all make suggestions for literature or further reading that will help you to firm up your ideas and arguments.

Some students are nervous about speaking in lectures and seminars and engaging with debates; they don't want to come across as silly or wrong. It can feel daunting putting your ideas 'out there' in the open space of the seminar room. To overcome this, you can help yourself by preparing for engaging with debates and discussions:

- Complete any preparatory seminar readings or tasks that have been set by the lecturer or seminar tutor;
- As well as making notes on the preparatory tasks, make some notes on what your thoughts are about topic(s) that will be discussed – for example, can you relate to the topic(s) experientially as well as with the literature?;
- Practise verbalizing your ideas in advance and what literature you can draw on to support your points(s);
- Practise with friends/peers in smaller informal study groups;
- Remember that feeling apprehensive about expressing ideas in front of others is very common – you won't be the only person in the room who needs to develop confidence doing this.

When you are in the teaching session, listen carefully to the contributions of your peers and make notes on what they are saying if you would like to. Ask yourself if you agree, or disagree and consider the reasons why you feel this way; what are your argument justifications? Are there any counter-argument justifications you can think of? What literature can you draw on? Remember you can take your time to consider the viewpoints in relation to the pre-session notes you have made. Now you're speaking up and engaging with the debate, remember to be courteous and respectful to the other speakers – being critical doesn't mean being negative or displaying unsupportive behaviours – listen to what they're saying and acknowledge their perspectives. Similar to the learners in Mercer's study you should engage with and encourage exploratory talk to ensure critical debate(s) in sessions.

ACTIVITY 5.2

Speaking in sessions

Reflection – have a think about the reasons why you want to speak in teaching sessions. Some students do not feel ready or able to speak in them. If you're one of these students, thinking about why you'd like to speak (even if you feel unable to at the moment) may help you to find your voice.

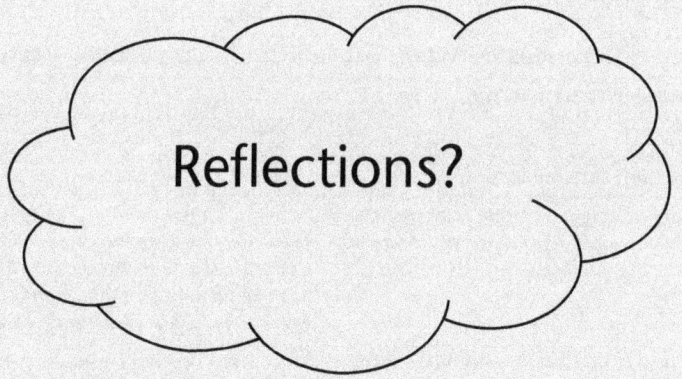

Some of the reasons you have identified may include:

- An enjoyment in talking and engaging with different ideas;
- Wanting to share your interests and ideas;
- An opportunity to try out and rehearse ideas in a 'safe' space with your lecturers and peers;
- Challenging yourself to think of a response to the discussion – this can be a good indication of your thinking and if you need to develop this further.

Presenting critical thinking with spoken communication

Presenting critical thinking verbally requires you to construct an argument. At first, the argument construction process for spoken communication is the same as if you were presenting an argument for written communication. Similarly to a written argument, you need to present an argument to persuade your listeners, whether that's an audience with you in the same room or an individual listening to a podcast or watching a documentary later. Please refer back to Chapter 4 to remind yourself of this process.

Once the arguments have been constructed, you need to consider the differences between written and spoken communication to ensure that the arguments and key messages are presented appropriately. Presenting your ideas using spoken communication is different to written communication. There are many different types of written and spoken assessment tasks and some of the key differences are noted in the table below.

Key differences between presenting ideas verbally versus in a written format

Written communication	Spoken communication
The word count is usually longer e.g. 2,500 words – 5,000 words (longer for research projects).	Usually a shorter timeframe (e.g. a 15-minute presentation or podcast) or a poster combining visuals and words. It is often 'equivalent to' a word count. Ask your lecturers if you're not sure.
There is space within the word count to take the time to set the context and indulge the reader in this.	There is the need to be succinct – you only have a short timeframe to present the key messages and arguments.
Within an essay you can build and develop complex arguments: the reader is going to follow and 'spend' more time with you and your voice.	Messages and arguments need to be more impactful and you need to make your point clearly – time is limited!
There is a focus on the written – sentence structure and grammatical impact. These need to be correct so the messages/arguments are clear for the reader to see and understand.	The visual content or key messages and overall impact of the presentation/podcast is important.
Your voice and tone within the text and the flow of your writing are important.	The tone, pace and delivery of the messages/arguments are important.
Written work can be re-read and the reader can go back to points for clarification if they don't understand a point first time.	Unless recorded, the audience only has one chance to hear and understand.

Planning for spoken communication

The planning and style of delivery required will vary depending on the type of assessment. For example, a presentation requires a formal voice, but a podcast may have a conversational voice, a more relaxed tone to help engage the other speakers and audience.

With the key differences identified, it is clear to see how important it is to plan a presentation, poster or podcast accordingly – you have as much to say as you would if you were writing an assignment, but only have a limited amount of time to do this, visual aids (if any) may need consideration, and there may be only one chance for delivery (if it is not being recorded). It will be different with a podcast, but even so you need to aim to make sure that the arguments and key messages are clear and the audience understands your points the first time around.

Similarly to the written format, it is important to present your critical voice in verbal communication. It should be **your** voice and what **you** want to say. As we have discussed in previous chapters, once you have completed your reading and research and started to engage critically with the topic area, you can decide on your argument(s), key points to support these, and the relevant literature to strengthen these. Ask yourself 'what do I want to say?'. This is an important question because it will mean that your work and your voice is authentic. It will help you to speak passionately about the topic and the audience will consider the verbal communication as more credible and authentic. To put more of yourself in the verbal communication, try to use stories or real-life illustrations when giving examples. These can be anecdotal and should also be supported with relevant literature.

ACTIVITY 5.3

How would you persuade someone?

Reflecting on the strategies to build an argument in Chapter 4 and the components of critical thinking in spoken communication listed in the previous table this chapter, what would you need to do to deliver a persuasive talk? What key elements would it need to contain?

Structure

The structure of a presentation can follow a similar structure for written communication. It usually has an introduction, main body and conclusion. In spoken communication, this can look like:

- Introduction – tell the audience what the focus is.
    You should provide the thesis statement (the argument connected to the assignment's focus) and signposting for the audience. Tell them what your main argument is and how you're going to present it. This will avoid the audience becoming 'lost' when the arguments/perspectives are presented and discussed. They will know what you're presenting and why?
- Main body – tell the audience about the focus;
    In the main body part of the presentation, develop and present the argument again, now taking the time to explain and unpack the argument. Every point should be clearly made and evidenced. You can use the PEEL model (similar to written communication):
- (State) Point;
- Explain with some description and evidence;
- Evaluate with evidence;
- Link to next point in argument.
- Conclusion – summarize and tell the audience what you told them, leaving them with a memorable point.

In this part, remind the audience of the key arguments (briefly) and how they were supported with evidence. At the end of the piece, give the audience a memorable statement to close it. It could be a question if it is a podcast or an impactful visual if it is a presentation along with a question. The conclusion is the final section where you can ensure your spoken communication stands out and has impact. The audience should also be thanked for taking the time to listen and asked if they have any questions. The Q&A part of a presentation is another opportunity for you to demonstrate critical thinking.

Using evidence critically and effectively in your spoken communication

Visual aids, for example a slide deck in PowerPoint, a Prezi or a handout, can be used to support your verbal communication. Within them you can provide the audience with evidence from the literature that can be provided as supporting evidence, photographs and pictures, tables, charts and graphs. They can help to communicate the key messages and make the points more memorable.

> **Looking to the future**
>
>
>
> MacFarlane (2018: 1201) suggests '**sudent success** in higher education is dependent upon the **possession of a positive learner identity**'.
>
> I will:
> – Perceive myself as a learner;
> – Complete preparatory tasks in advance of sessions;
> – Read at least one additional piece of wider reading for each module each week.

Figure 5.1   Example of a visual aid

The visual aid should be succinct, and the messages should be clear (see Figure 5.1). They should be used to enhance the communication. One way to do this is to provide key words and evidence relevant to the point being discussed at that time. You could also use a bold font and a different colour or provide an image so that the audience remembers this point.

The use and type of visuals that are expected or acceptable in a presentation will differ depending on the context – take time to check in with the assessment information to clarify what you can or cannot use. Also **remember the needs of your audience** when considering visuals: will there be anyone with specific needs that you might make adjustments for? For example, good practice for some learners with a specific learning difficulty (such as dyslexia) can include spacing out text, using clear headings or bold sections and presenting information in bullet points. This clear and accessible approach to how you present information usually helps *all* learners along the way. If part of your presentation includes a video clip, make sure this has subtitles because this helps people if English isn't their first language, or if they are deaf or hearing impaired. There are lots more ideas about making your presentation materials accessible on the website, Designing for Diverse learners: https://designingfordiverselearners.info

Techniques to develop the skill of spoken communication and connect with your audience

Developing effective communication is a skill. Some students may feel more prepared to do it than others, but everyone can deliver spoken communication with some tips and techniques. In a way, deciding what the arguments and key points are and how to present them structurally are the more challenging tasks. However, we understand that for some students the verbal communication (speaking) part is the most challenging. Now we're going to look at some techniques to help with such challenges. There are other ways you can connect with your audience – visual representations, articulation, tone, pace and space. It's also important to give your audience time to think: this means that you always have time for a moment to take pressure off yourself and take a pause.

Visual representations e.g. photographs depicting metaphorical images are important and can help to engage your audience. When using visual representations consider the way that the audience will see them and the impact they will have. They should not distract the audience from the key points being presented. It can be quite tempting to add lots of bright colours and moving parts, but with this in mind, avoid using animations, transitions and unnecessary sound effects. Any colours or images should be used to emphasize a point and make it stand out, having a lasting impact on the audience.

Articulation, the way in which you express yourself, your thoughts and ideas and pronounce your words is a key communication skill and central to an effective presentation. Clear pronunciation of words means that you can clearly tell your story and get the ideas across to the audience with clear meaning and understanding.

Tone and whether we talk passionately and excitedly in the presentation or in a bored and disinterested way can also have an impact on the way in which the audience connects with you and the talk. Try to talk enthusiastically and passionately about the topic so that the audience wants to share in this. You can also emphasize particular words and phrases to convey their significance by using a different tone of voice.

Pace and **space** in a similar way can also help to engage the audience. With verbal communication it's important to give the audience time to listen to what is being said, hear it, then take it in and understand it. As we mentioned earlier in the chapter, one of the key differences between written and verbal communication is that in written communication the reader can go back and revisit any points for clarification. This isn't possible with verbal communication (unless it is recorded). Make use of pauses to ensure the audience can listen to and process the information. You can also emphasize key words and phrases that are central to the talk with your voice and make use of colour and visual aids so that they are rememberable.

The speed at which you deliver your words is also very significant: speeding through words (often while looking down and reading them directly) is a clear indication to the audience (including those assessing you) that you would have probably benefited from greater rehearsal and more knowledge of the material you are delivering. Slow down and take the time to look up at your listeners and make brief eye contact with someone in the audience every now and again. If this feels too intimidating, look to the wall at the back of the room – this is still much better than looking down all the time.

Audience participation can also be used as a way to connect with the audience. At different points in the verbal communication you can involve the audience by asking them questions or giving them short tasks. Activities can help indicate to you that the audience are still engaged and help you to feel encouraged and positive in your delivery. Useful audience participation techniques can range from a simple show of hands in a kind of 'vote' to more interactive activities such as polls, quizzes or collection of ideas via various apps audience members might use on their phones. It depends on the nature of your presentation, the room layout and other resources available to you.

Overcoming nerves

Audiences at university are generally very supportive – your peers and lecturers want you to deliver strong verbal communication and succeed, and they understand that presenters experience a range of nerves. Despite knowing this, some students do experience nerves when they are required to speak and present. A few nerves are to be expected – communicating work verbally, 'putting it out there' can be daunting because we're not sure how the audience will receive it and what questions or feedback they may have. We would be surprised if students said they weren't nervous. However, sometimes nerves can be counterproductive in the preparation and delivery of presentations and other forms of spoken communication. Students often find strategies such as practising and using cue cards can help if they do find themselves nervous.

Practise the presentation to yourself. If you're able to it helps to do this in front of a mirror. You can practise the timing of the presentation overall and make a note of how long you're spending on the introduction, main arguments and the conclusion. Are you spending too much time introducing the argument? You can also reflect on whether the arguments and points made are supported with enough evidence. Do you find yourself talking really fast and racing to the end to make sure you can quickly conclude? If you find you're either talking too slowly or too quick, you need to revisit your planning and consider adding or taking points from the argument. You can also practise delivering in terms of the articulation of words, the tone, pace and your body language. Are you speaking in an engaging way that the audience will want to listen to and are you leaving enough pauses so that they can hear and comprehend your main points and overall arguments? There are lots of resources available to support you with developing these skills, for example Caroline Goyder's TEDxBrixton talk 'The surprising secret to speaking with confidence' https://tinyurl.com/bd9wfbvv and Amy Cuddy's TEDGlobal talk 'Your body language may shape who you are' https://tinyurl.com/43be2dfu. If you have access to Powerpoint you can use 'Rehearse your slide show with Speaker Coach' https://tinyurl.com/44wfhp66. It will help you to review aspects of your presentation such as timing, pacing and pitch, tone and language.

ACTIVITY 5.4

Practise presenting ideas

Go to a media source e.g. the BBC website or *The Guardian* and read an article. Try to pick a topic you have some knowledge of or where you have strong views. Write a script with the necessary characteristics of critical thinking: How would you summarize the key arguments of the article? What aspects of the article do you agree with and disagree with? Can you think of some literature to evidence your points? Record yourself presenting the script and then listen back to it. Do your arguments come across to you as a listener? Is there anything you would add or remove?

You could also present the script to your peers in a critical friend group. Questions for discussion within the peer group could include:

- What is or are the main argument(s)?
- Is or are the argument(s) clearly presented?
- What strategies have been used to build the argument(s)?
- Do the points come across clearly?

Working in groups and discussing questions like these will be helpful for the presenter and the students who are listening and being the audience. Being able to think critically about the script will enable the listening students to articulate the key strategies for argument development.

Students can often use cue cards or notes in presentations. These can provide a sense of safety; in case they forget their words. However, try to only write key words and phrases to support the talk. If there are many notes, it's likely they will be on large pieces of paper and if someone is nervous and shaking, this will show the audience that this is the case. If using cue cards, use smaller size paper or card (the thicker the paper/card the less movement from shaking and nerves will be visible).

Summing up

Engaging with debates in seminars can help to significantly develop, practise and rehearse ideas and critical thinking. Engaging in opportunities like these to practise your spoken communication offers the chance to develop your skills and confidence.

Presenting critical thinking verbally requires you to construct an argument. At first, the argument construction process for spoken communication is the same as if you were presenting an argument for written communication. It's important to consider the format of the communication e.g. oral presentation, documentary or podcast and the audience.

References

Cuddy, A. (2012), *Your Body Language May Shape Who You Are*. Available at: https://www.youtube.com/watch?v=Ks-_Mh1QhMcTEDGlobal (accessed 29 September 2024).

Goyder, C. (2018), *The Surprising Secret to Speaking with Confidence*. Available at: https://www.youtube.com/watch?v=a2MR5XbJtXUTEDXBrixton. (accessed 29 September 2024).

Heron, M. (2019), 'Pedagogic Practices to Support International Students in Seminar Discussions', *Higher Education Research & Development*, 38 (2): 266–79.

Mercer, N. (2000), *Words and Minds: How We Use Language to Think Together*, London: Routledge.

Vygotsky, L. (1968), *Thought and Language*, Cambridge, MA: MIT Press.

CHAPTER 6

How to Reflect Critically

Reflection: what does this word bring to mind? It is certainly one where there could be many differing definitions. It is also a term that is seen and used frequently in the discipline of Education: a common, embedded practice for educators, and a concept that students of Education will need to work with.

This chapter will enable you to gain a greater understanding of critical reflection via;

- Exploring **different models of reflective practice** from both the perspective of the learner and the teacher.
- Considering **how we engage in reflective practice** and what this might look like in reality in written work.
- Identifying **characteristics of critical reflection in writing**.

What *is* reflection?

Reflection is one characteristic of Education that makes it a unique discipline compared to many other social science subjects. Farrell (2012: 8) noted that 'the terms reflection and reflective practice are so popular in education that they are nearly mandatory'.

Reflecting upon our own educational experiences is often the route into our educational enquiry or the starting point to explore an issue, for example, how do our own schooling experiences differ with those of someone historically? What do we recall as the best characteristics of the teachers we liked the most? Understanding the concept of reflection and applying it is integral to critical thinking in our discipline, and applying this to ourselves, as learners, or as educators, can take some getting used to. Self-reflection can sometimes feel somewhat forced or laden with fears about 'getting it right', but the beauty of reflection is that while some reflection can be more effective and valuable than others, there isn't a right or wrong answer. And, practising self-reflection can really pay off.

A general **definition of reflection** that you would find in a dictionary focuses upon the mirror-like associations we have with the word, i.e. what we are viewing and the way we receive, or think about this. There is an emphasis upon something being *sent back* to us, and then what we do with this. And, just as we may look in the mirror and decide we need to take action to rectify an element of our appearance (for example, brushing our hair), when we engage in reflective practice, we can identify what might need to be altered.

> As reflective Education students, **it is the way in which we receive what is 'sent back' to us – and what we do with this that we need to work with** to enact critical reflection. Reflection isn't just thinking: **there needs to be action about the thinking and an intention to learn as a result of this. It is thinking about something, for a purpose, and identifying change that has occurred as a result of this.**

ACTIVITY 6.1

Turning writing into critically reflective writing

Part 1: Set a two-minute timer (be strict) and write a passage about your recollections of a school project, or the first time you completed an assignment at college or university. Try to 'freewrite' here without worrying about the quality too much. Focus upon recounting the experience, and try to write continually for the whole two minutes, without stopping.

When you have completed this, resist the temptation to correct/amend/improve it for now. We'll come back to work further on this piece of writing later in the chapter.

What shapes reflection?

Early educational theory around reflection points commonly to the work of John Dewey (1859–1952) and Donald Schön (1930–97). Dewey usefully reminds us of the need for 'careful consideration of any belief or supposed form of knowledge' (1910: 6) which epitomizes a critical thinking approach perfectly and should be applied to our own thoughts and experiences, not just information created by others.

The experiences we have lead us to develop certain beliefs: what might be referred to as ontological assumptions, i.e. things that shape

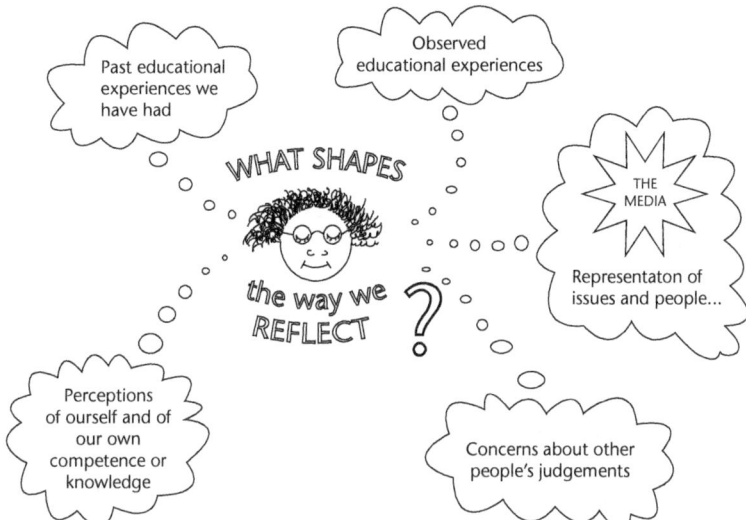

Figure 6.1 What shapes the way we reflect?

the views we have of the world, and certain issues we encounter. These beliefs then impact upon the way we think about and reflect upon issues and experiences. For example, an adult who had a lack of support with special educational needs at school, which led to negative experiences and outcomes, might believe that the education system, and even education itself is of little value.

Consider what kinds of experiences or factors in your life have contributed to the way you might reflect upon things. Perhaps you could annotate the illustration in Figure 6.1, add notes and further comments to think about what aspects of your life may have led you to reflect upon issues and ideas in a certain way?

Models of reflection

It's useful to know about different models of reflection to help you think about the most effective reflective approaches for you and your needs and to recognize that there are strengths and limitations to different approaches (we need to reflect critically upon approaches to reflection!). This next section works with some of the most popular models of reflection within our discipline.

You will come across these models during your study of Education, and you will see that often they share common ideas (the application of some of these is discussed in the next chapter when thinking about being critical in practice).

Bear in mind that the approaches below were developed at different periods in time (important due to the influences on particular thinking in some disciplines historically), with different learners, or roles, in mind, and so while we could identify and discuss differences, there isn't an easy and straightforward comparison – or judgement of which is 'best' – that could be made.

Some have a greater emphasis upon describing **what** has happened and thinking this through, whereas others prompt greater **evaluation** i.e. trying to make judgements and seek possible explanations as to why things have happened, and the consequences of this. All are forward thinking (remember, 'action'), with an emphasis upon encouraging the identification of what to do again in similar situations, whether that is to replicate behaviour that led to a success or make changes to improve an experience in the future. Below is an outline of five key models of reflection, and some of the core characteristics of each.

Boud (1985): With colleagues Keogh and Walker, Boud developed a **three-stage model** for reflection, and the descriptors they use to characterize each stage are incredibly useful when we are thinking about feelings that might be encountered during the reflective process. Their model begins with three core elements which are preparation, engagement, and finally processing, then, as the image associated with their model (Figure 6.2) demonstrates, the reflective element is divided into the experience, the reflective process and the outcome.

This model emphasizes that during the experience, there is little time to think about or process what is occurring, and that productive reflection requires structure in order to help make connections, reconstruct the experience and identify the gains. They emphasize that 'reflection is pursued ... with intent' (Boud, Keogh and Walker, 1985: 11) and so is purposeful and deliberate. An example that many students could relate to here is an experience in class, or a seminar, where a difficult situation has been encountered, such as not being able to make contributions where expected, or struggling with understanding material. The feelings associated with this might be embarrassment or discomfort. This might then create a reluctance to return to that class or situation. Using Boud's model above would require acknowledging and returning to the significant feelings attached to that experience, and

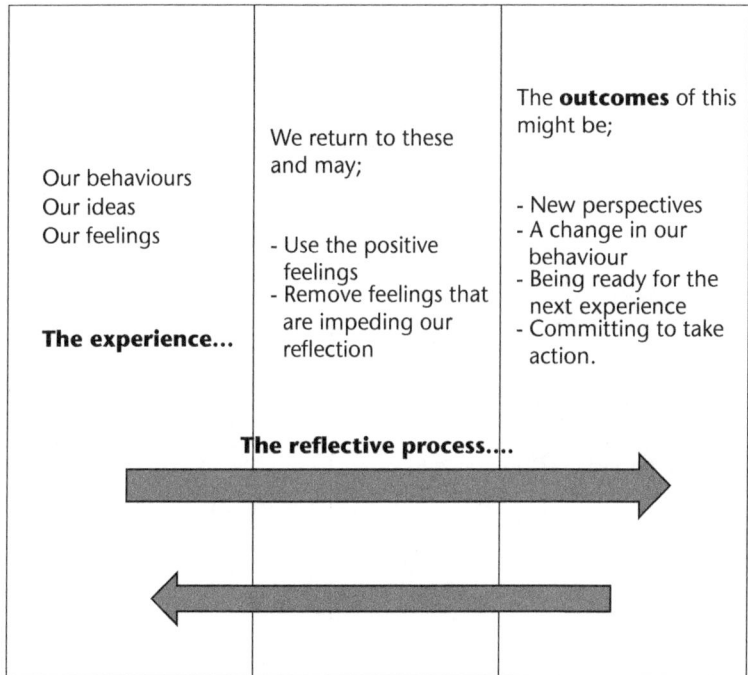

Figure 6.2 The Reflective Process, adapted from Boud, Keogh and Walker (1985)

working with those feelings to contribute to an evaluation of the experience: making some kind of judgement or conclusion about the reasons behind these feelings. This might lead to developing a new perspective (such as valuing and prioritizing preparation for class in study plans) and a commitment to action this in the future via time management.

Kolb (1984): Presented most popularly in a circular, clockwise graphic, there are four key stages in Kolb's **experiential learning cycle**, beginning with a Concrete Experience, which cycles through to a Reflective Observation, followed by some Abstract Conceptualization, and ending with Active Experimentation in the future. Kolb's model is clearly situated in the classical thinking of, amongst others, John Dewey, Lev Vygotsky and Jean Piaget, all influential theorists whose names you have no doubt come across in your studies. The basic premise and stages of Kolb's cycle can be seen in Figure 6.3, as a visual representation.

96 Critical Thinking for Education Students

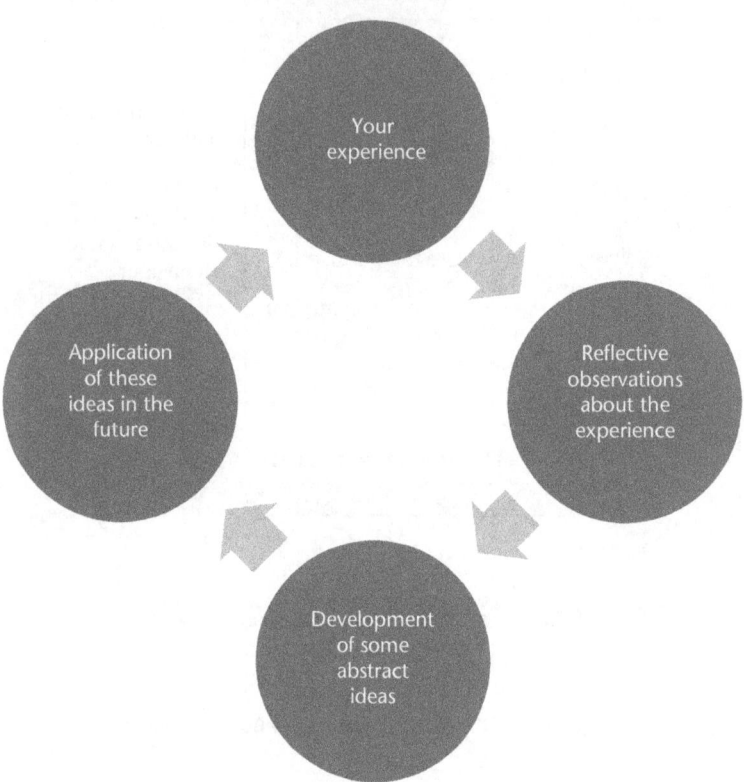

Figure 6.3   Adapted from Kolb (1984)

This model emphasizes that it is the **transformation** of experiences, i.e. how we can convert an instance or occasion into something to take forward purposefully. You may come across references to Kolb's learning style inventory, this is a tool that was developed to help learners identify the way they learn from experiences and has been extensively used across the world and updated several times. Consider a young child learning about abstract concepts such as volume and measurement or liquid, playing with water and containers in their classroom. Their concrete experience would comprise playing with water, pouring it from one container into another, and noticing the effects of this (e.g. overflowing water). The reflective observation here involves the child thinking about what they have observed, and trying to understand the reasons for this, particularly drawing upon existing knowledge or experience of similar situations. The abstract conceptualization phase is where they might recognize a new idea about the notion of volume or measurement, and then form a kind of 'rule' about such an instance in their head, such as what looks like the tallest and longest container doesn't actually hold the most water. The active experimentation phase here would be taking this principle forward and testing it out with other containers, and in the future in other similar situations around measurement, quantities and volume.

Gibbs (1988): Graham Gibbs developed this more detailed cycle of reflective practice which is encapsulated by the title of his book, *Learning by Doing*. Gibbs asserted that simply having an experience by itself was not enough to enact and embed learning, and that reflection is needed in order to identify feelings and thoughts, which can then be taken forward into generalizations which can be applied to new situations. You can see how closely this reflects the basic ideas of Kolb and Boud above, but Gibbs' cycle has six stages which expands upon these, and attributes more time to **describing** an experience, and the **thoughts and feelings** attached to this:

1 Description

2 Thoughts and Feelings

3 Evaluation

4 Analysis

5 Conclusion

6 Action Plan

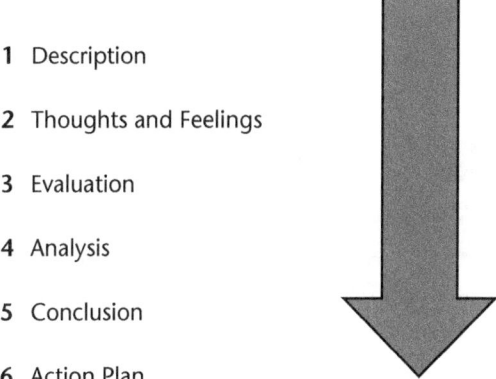

An example here might be a learner giving a presentation, where nerves and anxious feelings impacted upon their delivery. Their description of the presentation might be quite detailed, with a chronological story to be told about what they did and in what order. Their thoughts and feelings might be quite emotive, feeling fearful, which could have been seen through rushing their words, rustling notes due to feelings of panic, and perhaps relief but also disappointment afterwards. Evaluating this experience requires making some kind of judgement, and the student might apply various kinds of criteria to themselves here, looking to the reactions of the audience, tutor, or the grade they received. The analysis phase is subtly different: this is taking a small step back from the description and emotions, and various measures of success. Analysis requires breaking the experience down into component parts to better understand it. In this instance, the student might think back to some of the reasons that contributed to the performance they gave, such as identifying the extent to which they were prepared, what elements of the presentation were stronger than others, and trying to achieve a better understanding of the situation and experience as a whole. All of these elements then combine to allow the student to come to a conclusion, such as recognizing that, overall, the presentation was not a positive experience, and they don't want to be in that same situation again. Finally, the action plan phase impresses upon us the importance of articulating and documenting intentions for the future, not just having a vague notion or idea of what *might* be a good idea to do next time. So in this instance the student could identify concrete and tangible actions which might include starting the work earlier, having a tutorial to get early feedback on their ideas, doing more rehearsals, taking the time to do some mindfulness or calm breathing before delivery, and slowing their voice down.

> **ACTIVITY 6.1**
>
> ### Turning writing into critically reflective writing (continued)
>
> **Part 2:** Touch base again with the example that you were asked to free-write about earlier in this chapter, the experience of a project or assignment.
>
> Now choose one of the three models (Boud, Kolb or Gibbs) outlined above, and apply this to that experience. Use the space below to sketch out the diagram for whichever model you choose, then annotate this with features of your own experience. It doesn't matter what it looks like – it's something just for you to work on, individually.

> **Reflection**
>
> - The first point of reflection here is, why did you choose the model you worked with?
>
> - What made you reject the others?
>
> - How did you find the process of taking an unstructured piece of free-writing and re-working it into a model?
>
> - What did you identify at the end as a way to go forward?
>
> - Can you think of other circumstances or situations you encounter where applying this model (or similar) will develop your critical and reflective thinking further?

The last two models outlined below are slightly different in that they are more focused upon the use of reflection from a practitioners' perspective – usually that of a teacher. They are included here to illustrate two things:

- The **difference** in reflective practice depending upon whether it is being implemented from the point of view as a teacher, or a learner.
- The **similarities** in reflective practice, regardless as to whether this is being implemented from the point of view as a teacher, or a learner!

Come back up to this space when you have read the models below and see if you have been able to identify any of the similarities and differences between these different kinds of models (those for the learner, and those for the teacher).

Schön (1983): Specific to educational practitioners, the ideas of **knowing in action** (doing something habitually without thinking about it), **reflection in action** (as you go along) and **reflection on action** (deliberate and intentional exercise after an event or experience) stem from the work of Donald Schön, in this book *The Reflective Practitioner*. These ideas recognize that reflection is, can, and should be spontaneous, but that it is also something we need to put effort into and plan for. A frequently cited quote from Schön's book is that in such instances where an individual is pausing to reflect, 'the practitioner allows himself to experience surprise, puzzlement, or confusion in a situation … he reflects upon the phenomena before him, and on the prior understandings which have been implicit in his behaviour' (1983: 68). This emphasizes the significance of what we know – or what we *think* we know – before a situation, and how an experience and our reflection on this can change and re-shape our understanding.

For a teacher, the model might be observed as simply as;

- Knowing in action – subconsciously and naturally nodding as a learner gives feedback, to encourage their input.
- Reflection in action – scanning a group of learners and noticing which have not yet contributed to a discussion or answered a question.
- Reflection on action – considering if a different approach in the same situation might encourage more participation from those who struggle to join in.

Brookfield (1995): This model was developed specifically with the reflective practice of teachers in mind, from Brookfield's perspective as an adult educator. It uses the concept of **looking through different lenses** to reflect upon an experience. The premise behind this is expressed by Brookfield as he says, 'no matter how much we think we have a full and accurate picture of our practice we're always stymied [hindered] by our personal limitations' (1995: 61). This starting point recognizes that to engage in reflection we often need to consider it from a point of view external to ourselves, and that this is particularly valuable for teachers to allow them to illuminate aspects of their practice. Each of these lenses is as outlined below:

1 The **Autobiographical lens** (the self). Brookfield acknowledges that the value of our own experience and viewpoint has often been downplayed as anecdotal, or too subjective, but that personal experiences – particularly those teachers had as learners themselves – are often a key factor in shaping a teaching approach. Acknowledging this can be constructive in identifying assumptions, for example thinking that what worked for us will automatically work for our learners, which of course is not always the case.
2 The Client, Learner, or **Student lens**. In any kind of pedagogical situation (e.g. teaching in a classroom, or a one-to-one tutorial), the learner can be receiving, or perceiving, a very different message and experience to that which was intended by the teacher. This is unique to each learner too, in that every individual can be having a different experience of the same lesson. For Brookfield, one of the key ways to tap into this is to enable anonymous student feedback to try and understand the varying ways students view the teachers' practice.
3 The Co-worker, or **Colleague lens**. A colleague can be a trusted critical friend who has a shared understanding of the experiences of a fellow teacher and can empathize and relate to challenges and victories experienced in the classroom. Equally, an insight into the co-workers' lens can bring a different perspective to light.

Opportunities for reflection with colleagues, either in structured meetings, or through incidental conversations can confirm that experiences are shared, and not specific to the individual, which is reassuring for the practitioner.
4 The **Theoretical lens.** This final approach to viewing practice reminds practitioners that they need to keep returning to theories, ideas and literature to refresh, re-engage or reset their practices. Brookfield says that 'reading theory can sometimes feel like coming home' (1995: 73), meaning that returning to the roots of what was learned can be reaffirming, reassuring, or remind practitioners of useful values and approaches, which can prompt or engender critical reflection.

You will find many more models about reflection or reflective practice in your learning, and possibly throughout your career and any professional development learning you undertake. Take note of the ways in which they build upon and develop existing ideas from models that have gone before them, and the similar themes and ideas that are apparent amongst them. Hopefully you can see from the brief overview of the five models above that the practice of reflection, by its very nature, requires you to be **querying, curious,** *open to a range of views,* and *thinking about next steps*: all part of being a critical student of Education.

How to engage in reflective practice

Note the key word in the title here: **practice**. To become a more critical thinker, we can practise (keep repeating) reflection in lots of different situations: this helps it to become a habitual event, something we do regularly.

The key message here is that to effectively engage in reflective practice, your **reflection needs to be captured,** so that you can re-visit it, documented or recorded in some way, and build upon the gems that were your thoughts from a particular moment in time, to further your learning and development.

Writing down **notes** or using a **diagram** such as those created by one of the models above is a good starting point. There are lots of blank templates online if you want to have a structure to adhere to, or you could just create your own, taking the headings from the models above that resonate most for you. Remember that essentially the essence of them is:

1 What have I experienced?
2 What was that like?

3 What have I learned?
4 What would I do next time?

A quicker and more accessible way for you to capture your thoughts and reflections might be by recording some audio notes, recalling your ideas verbally and recording them onto your phone or another device.

> **TIP**
>
> The most important thing to remember is to **record your thoughts in a timely way** – don't rely on your memory to conjure up how you felt about a certain situation two months later.

If you like to capture ideas more graphically or work in a more visual way, any kind of **illustration, mind map** or **diagram** that makes sense to you is also a valid way to capture your critical reflection. Perhaps **photos** you take will also form part of your reflections (be sure to check policies around taking photos in any kind of educational setting, as this may be prohibited in relation to safeguarding policies). For example, if you are setting up a learning activity or lesson using resources, the 'before' photo of carefully curated and laid out resources will always look very different to the 'after' photo, which might show that learners engaged with an activity in a totally different manner to the way you envisaged in your careful planning, and this could form a valuable piece of evidence or data to inform your reflection about how you might do the activity again in the future.

In summary, in situations where critical reflection is required of you, remember these **four key elements**:

1 Use some kind of **structure**, key words or template (you could experiment with which approach or diagram works best for you, and these may be different depending upon the situation).
2 **Capture your ideas as soon as possible** after the experience. This might be with some quick written notes, or might include a range of media. Some journalling apps allow you to collect photos, links, videos, voice memos and written notes together in one place, which might help to provide you with a rich collection of stimuli to draw upon when analysing and using these reflections.
3 Put aside time to return to them and **add more** in-depth reflection, explanations and analysis of your experiences afterwards.
4 Be sure to articulate and **record the action or intention** you plan to take forward as a result of your reflections.

Showcasing critical thinking in your assessments

Oftentimes, the learning outcomes attached to a particular assignment will require you to evidence your critical thinking, or reflection, in relation to practice, for example while on a placement, observing learners, or as part of your own learning experience. You will be well equipped to do so if you can follow the four practical tips above to ensure that you have the kinds of evidence you need to substantiate your reflections and have this to present or refer to in your academic work.

The kinds of terminology you might come across could ask you to;

> 'Critically reflect upon the relevance of your observations in relation to ...'

> 'Critically reflect upon learning experiences and the impact of these upon ...'

> 'Critically reflect upon challenges associated with the implementation of ...'

The most common type of error students tend to make when faced with a task such as this is to invest too much time in describing observations or experiences, at the cost of analysis and critical reflection. Below is a fairly extensive example in response to the question posed, asking the learner to reflect upon their observations and link these to policy. It illustrates the component parts of the 'critical reflection' process that will help to demonstrate your more sophisticated and critical response to meeting the learning outcome.

ACTIVITY 6.2

Identifying characteristics of critical reflection

After reading the excerpt below, think about the following questions:

1 Can you identify which sections might align with common phases of the models presented earlier in the chapter?

2 Write down a few key words in the right-hand margin that identify what stage of reflection the writer is engaged in.

3 How might you encourage them to be more critical in their thinking in their reflections?

See some suggested responses to these questions after the excerpt, and also a worked example at the end of the chapter.

ACTIVITY 6.3

Critically reflect upon your observations in relation to contemporary policy within your setting

Margin for your notes

Within the early years setting where I have spent the last three months on placement, the impact of changing government policy and practice has become very apparent as a result of my observations over time, my research into the area, and also my conversations with practitioners and parents. The reflection below focuses upon one particular instance where I was able to analyse the impact of macro-level economic concerns all the way down to the micro level of the relationships between one particular child and his carer. It has really stayed with me as a very emotional and memorable moment and encapsulates the complexity of early years settings as a place of connections and safety and key foundations for young children.

In early 2024, early years providers were subject to a change to the EYFS (Early Years Foundation Stage) which was updated (DfE, 2024). These changes included alterations to qualifications that should be held by practitioners and changes to staff: child ratios, that is the number of staff needed to care for the children. These were requirements for Early Years (EY) settings to implement amongst the backdrop of a UK childcare context with complex changes to funding for parents which are not financially sustainable for many nurseries, and an ever-increasing number of EY settings closing (Ofsted, 2023). On a macro level, these changes have resulted in a great many discussions about the health of the sector (TES, 2024) and in particular, difficulties in recruiting staff (EECC, 2023).

Whilst on placement, even in the short space of three months whilst I was there, I was aware of turnover in the staff body. I spoke to two new apprentices who expressed their love for working with young children but were uncertain if it would be their 'forever career' (see diary, p. 23). There was also the departure of a long-standing member of staff who was clearly held in high regard by the parents, but was leaving in order to move sectors entirely, because she had been at a pay ceiling for many years, and also needed more flexibility in her working hours. These changes caused concern to parents with regards to stability and consistency of care for their children (see diary p. 31). For the children attending the setting, the practice of keyworkers (a practice grounded in the concept or attachment to caregivers, stemming from the work of Bowlby, 1954) was also disrupted by these changes, and this was something I observed in a particularly memorable moment in the pre-school room of the nursery, with children in the age group of three and four years old.

The children had been informed that their practitioner, Denise (pseudonym), would be leaving for a new job. This had been carefully managed with stories about moving on, capturing memories and pictures of their time with Denise, and conversations about new adventures. It tied in well, in many ways, to conversations around transitions and moving onto primary school for these children. The children had also enjoyed a farewell party with Denise, and parents had been well informed about the staff changes. On Denise's last day, when many children were being collected by parents, they were visibly sad about her leaving. For the most part this was temporary and manageable, but for one child in particular, their departure with Denise resulted in very acute and prolonged distress. This was really upsetting for everyone involved and it took a great deal of time from the adults involved to help the child regulate their emotions, move to a different corner of the nursery, and say Goodbye to Denise and then leave calmly. I observed lots of comforting, acknowledgement of the child's feelings as valid, and sharing of feelings from the adults about their sadness too.

It was a really interesting experience for me to observe this whole interaction as a commendable example of love and care for a young child and their feelings. This required knowledge of child psychology, child development, and the cumulative experience of many years from the parent and practitioners involved. It was apparent to see that the choice of words, actions and the pace at which they engaged with the child was all very carefully and deliberately chosen. There was also the selection of the location, with the child's sensory needs taken into account, and cognisance of the impact of this distress upon other children considered. To the eyes of many observers, the complexity of the situation may have gone unnoticed, but the notes I captured afterwards (see diary, p. 32) where I reflected upon this, really uncovered the many layers of interactions that were at play in this one situation.

I reflected at the time that this was upsetting, and emotional for everyone involved. I really believe that the nursery put into place well-planned activities and interventions to help the children adjust to this change, and that the level of reaction and feeling from this one child could not have been anticipated by them. The day after, I chatted to the Deputy Manager about this and we shared our feelings about the situation. I told her that I felt I had learned a lot about how to support young children through transitions as a result of being involved in this time period, that it was a really positive insight for me and had piqued my interest in researching how to manage transitions for children. She said that the team would review the departure of staff at their next meeting to evaluate if what they had done prior to departure was sufficient, and whether they would do anything differently next time.

See the end of this chapter for some comments and suggestions on this worked example.

Summing up

Critical reflection can become a habit, and common practice that can improve your experiences in work settings and help you to become a more reflective practitioner. It is something particular to students of Education, and a process that can only be engaged in properly and meaningfully by real human beings – an AI assistant cannot generate individual and relevant reflections. While it becomes a natural way of working for educational practitioners, an ongoing and continual commitment to the explicit and intentional practice of reflection is also important. Adopting and applying common principles from different models of reflection can be a useful way to critically analyse experiences or issues that you may come across. The following chapter focuses upon behaviours, skills and the lifelong mindset of being a critical thinker in practice.

References

Boud, D., Keogh, R. and Walker, D. (1985), *Reflection: Turning Experience into Learning*, London: Kogan Page Ltd.

Bowlby, J. (1969 [1954]), *Attachment and Loss*, New York: Basic Books.

Brookfield, S. (1995), *Becoming a Critically Reflective Teacher*, San Francisco, CA: Jossey-Bass.

Department for Education (2024), *Early Years Foundation Stage Statutory Framework*. Available at: https://assets.publishing.service.gov.uk/media/670fa42a30536cb92748328f/EYFS_statutory_framework_for_group_and_school_-_based_providers.pdf (accessed 9 May 2025).

Dewey, J. (1910), *How We Think*, Boston, MA: D.C. Heath.

Early Education and Childcare Coalition (2023), *Retention and Return: Delivering the Expansion of Early Years Entitlement in England*. Available at: https://www.earlyeducationchildcare.org/early-years-workforce-report (accessed 9 May 2025).

Farrell, T. (2012), 'Reflecting on Reflective Practice: (Re)Visiting Dewey and Schön', *TESOL Journal*, 3: 7–16.

Gibbs, G. (1988), *Learning by Doing: A Guide to Teaching and Learning Methods*, London: Further Education Unit.

Hébert, C. (2015), 'Knowing and/or Experiencing: A Critical Examination of the Reflective Models of John Dewey and Donald Schön', *Reflective Practice*, 16 (3): 361–71, DOI:10.1080/14623943.2015.1023281

Kolb, D. (1984), *Experiential Learning: Experience as the Source of Learning Development*, Englewood Cliffs: Prentice Hall.

Ofsted (2023), *Main Findings: Childcare Providers and Inspections as at 31 March 2023*. Available at: https://www.gov.uk/government/statistics/childcare-providers-and-inspections-as-at-31-march-2023/main-findings-childcare-providers-and-inspections-as-at-31-march-2023#providers-registers (accessed 9 May 2025).

Schön, D. (1983), *The Reflective Practitioner: How Professionals Think in Action*, London: TempleSmith.

Times Educational Supplement (2024), *Warning Over 'Major Deterioration In Early Years Education*. Available at: https://www.tes.com/magazine/news/early-years/warning-deterioration-early-years-education (accessed 9 May 2025).

ACTIVITY 6.3

Worked example of an observation in practice

Critically reflect upon your observations in relation to contemporary policy within your setting.	Margin for your notes
Within the early years setting where I have spent the last three months on placement, the impact of changing government policy and practice has become very apparent as a result of my observations over time, my research into the area, and also my conversations with practitioners and parents. The reflection below focuses upon one particular instance where I was able to analyse the impact of macro-level economic concerns all the way down to the micro level of the relationships between one particular child and his carer. It has really stayed with me as a very emotional and memorable moment and encapsulates the complexity of early years settings as a place of connections and safety and key foundations for young children.	*Description, recounting experience (Boud)*
In early 2024, early years providers were subject to a change to the EYFS (Early Years Foundation Stage) which was updated (DfE, 2024). These changes included alterations to qualifications that should be held by practitioners and changes to staff: child ratios, that is the number of staff needed to care for the children. These were requirements for Early Years (EY) settings to implement amongst the backdrop of a UK childcare context with complex changes to funding for parents which are not financially sustainable for many nurseries, and an ever-increasing number of EY settings closing (Ofsted, 2022). On a macro level,	*Theoretical lens (Brookfield)* *Analysis (Gibbs) to understand how the situation arose.*

these changes have resulted in a great many discussions about the health of the sector (TES, 2024) and in particular, difficulties in recruiting staff (EECC, 2023).

Whilst on placement, even in the short space of three months whilst I was there, I was aware of turnover in the staff body. I spoke to two new apprentices who expressed their love for working with young children but were uncertain if it would be their 'forever career' (see diary, p. 23). There was also the departure of a long-standing member of staff who was clearly held in high regard by the parents, but was leaving in order to move sectors entirely, because she had been at a pay ceiling for many years, and also needed more flexibility in her working hours. These changes caused concern to parents with regards to stability and consistency of care for their children (see diary p.31). For the children attending the setting, the practice of keyworkers (a practice grounded in the concept or attachment to caregivers, stemming from the work of Bowlby, 1954) was also disrupted by these changes, and this was something I observed in a particularly memorable moment in the pre-school room of the nursery, with children in the age group of three and four years old.

The children had been informed that their practitioner, Denise (pseudonym), would be leaving for a new job. This had been carefully managed with stories about moving on, capturing memories and pictures of their time with Denise, and conversations about new adventures. It tied in well, in many ways, to conversations around transitions and moving onto primary school for these children. The children had also enjoyed a

Description (Boud)

Theoretical lens (Brookfield)

Evaluation of what practitioners had done to try and mitigate this beforehand (Boud, Gibbs)

farewell party with Denise, and parents had been well informed about the staff changes. On Denise's last day, when many children were being collected by parents, they were visibly sad about her leaving. For the most part this was temporary and manageable, but for one child in particular, their departure with Denise resulted in very acute and prolonged distress. This was really upsetting for everyone involved and it took a great deal of time from the adults involved to help the child regulate their emotions, move to a different corner of the nursery, and say Goodbye to Denise and then leave calmly. I observed lots of comforting, acknowledgement of the child's feelings as valid, and sharing of feelings from the adults about their sadness too.

Brookfield: lens of the learner (child)

It was a really interesting experience for me to observe this whole interaction as a commendable example of love and care for a young child and their feelings. This required knowledge of child psychology, child development, and the cumulative experience of many years from the parent and practitioners involved. It was apparent to see that the choice of words, actions and the pace at which they engaged with the child was all very carefully and deliberately chosen. There was also the selection of the location, with the child's sensory needs taken into account, and cognisance of the impact of this distress upon other children considered. To the eyes of many observers, the complexity of the situation may have gone unnoticed, but the notes I captured afterwards (see diary, p. 32) where I reflected upon this, really uncovered the many layers of interactions that were at play in this one situation.

Feelings and emotions (Boud)

Brookfield: lens of colleagues

Analysis (Gibbs) identifying the various component parts at play here.

I reflected at the time that this was upsetting, and emotional for everyone involved. I really believe that the nursery put into place-well planned activities and interventions to help the children adjust to this change, and that the level of reaction and feeling from this one child could not have been anticipated by them. The day after, I chatted to the Deputy Manager about this and we shared our feelings about the situation. I told her that I felt I had learned a lot about how to support young children through transitions as a result of being involved in this time period, that it was a really positive insight for me and had piqued my interest in researching how to manage transitions for children. She said that the team would review the departure of staff at their next meeting to evaluate if what they had done prior to departure was sufficient, and whether they would do anything differently next time.	Abstract conceptualization (Kolb) Action plan for the future (Gibbs)

Comment

There aren't right or wrong answers to the questions posed above, or the kinds of reflection you think can be seen in this excerpt. Hopefully you will be able to see the general structure which begins with setting the context, describing an event, analysing and reflecting on this, then some evaluation and forward thinking.

Some questions that might spring to mind in terms of encouraging greater critical thinking (question 3) could be;

- What was the writer themselves doing at the time of the incident they were observing?
- Can the writer identify any specific sources they have begun to research in order to learn more about transitions?

- Would explicitly applying Brookfield's model about the lenses of different individuals involved in this situation be helpful? For example, trying to identify and explore the feelings and views of others.
- Had the writer experienced any similar situations before, and was any judgement or bias at play?

Consider the 'critical questions' posed in Chapter 1 and whether applying these to this portion of writing could help the writer to improve the 'critical' element in their reflection. Asking How, Who, Why, Which, What and When can help to reveal further layers of reflection.

CHAPTER 7

How to Demonstrate Critical Thinking in Practice

Most of the content in this book has focused upon applying critical thinking in your current role as a student. Hopefully, it should be apparent to you that critical thinking is not something you leave behind when you complete your studies. Whatever the type of role or sector that you progress to, a habitual approach of trying to gain greater understanding via reflection, reasoning and scrutiny of evidence is a core skill for life.

This chapter will consider:

- Why critical thinking is a core **employability skill** valued highly by a range of employers (not just those in the education sector).
- **Critical thinking in real-world practical settings** and scenarios: for Education graduates, this may well be in educational settings.
- The importance of **engaging in professional development** and keeping knowledge of your sector up to date.
- How critical thinking is core to inclusion.

Critical thinking beyond university: it's a core employability skill

There are many reasons why employers want critical thinking skills within their teams, which include:

- They're crucial for **productive team working**; communicating, collaborating and negotiation are the processes through which progress is achieved and applying critical thinking in these conversations can help the development and stretching of ideas. This human interaction and production of new ideas and ways of working – informed by critical thinking – cannot be reproduced by AI.

- Having a habitual critical thinking approach can assist you in identifying bias, or questioning situations where injustices or indirect discrimination might be occurring. This is important for **diversity and inclusion** in all kinds of workplaces and helps to create a culture where we value others' lived experiences.
- Critical thinking is conducive to not making assumptions or jumping to conclusions – so when solutions are being sought, **evidence-based rational thinking is more likely to emerge**.
- In situations where analysis of data is required, being willing to not simply accept what is presented to you, and **question the provenance** of this (as discussed in Chapter 2) and methods behind the data (e.g. quantitative evidence on trends or performance) brings greater rigour to your work.
- If you are generating proposed actions, ways of working, or suggestions, thinking critically about questions people might ask helps to build a more **robust evidence base**.

Critical thinking in work-based settings

Demonstrating your critical thinking in a setting (such as a placement, work experience or during employment) is important for many reasons. This section identifies the reasons why critical thinking in a work-based setting is valuable, and that you can gain from adopting and evidencing a critical thinking approach in practice. Critical thinking can:

1 Build good relationships and make a positive impression

Presenting yourself as an enquiring individual can help to show that you are committed and interested in the setting, the practice and the people.

2 Maintain professional standards and obligations

Any kind of setting has certain expectations about behaviours and standards. For example, in an educational setting this could range from presenting yourself well around the school community with parents, to ensuring you fulfil your safeguarding responsibilities and report any issues of concern to a setting's Designated Safeguarding Lead (DSL), or equivalent. Reflecting critically upon yourself can help you to meet expectations in this way.

3 Develop you personally and professionally

Engaging with and being receptive to ideas you hear and practices you observe helps you to keep gaining more tacit knowledge which will contribute significantly to your ability to practice in specialized settings (think back to Brookfield's theoretical lens in the previous chapter here).

4 Deliver high-quality work or service in the setting

By taking an open-minded approach based on discussion and reflection we can consider how to improve the quality of our own actions and practice, and challenge assumptions that may be held. This in turn can lead to clarifications about expectations and ongoing reflection about the extent to which we are meeting these.

5 Question ideas, norms and practice you come across

It's OK to ask, 'Why?'. This is such a core part of critical thinking! 'Why is it done this way?' 'Why was this practice changed?' 'What are the reasons behind this?'. It's normal to feel a bit apprehensive asking questions, particularly if you perceive yourself as relatively inexperienced and you're asking these of someone you regard as an expert. However, remember that questioning and applying critical thinking in practice is a way that greater understanding can occur, it can encourage others' reflection, stimulate productive conversation, or shine light on poor evidence that is being used to justify a particular approach or practice.

> **Example: Professional criticality in an education setting**
>
> You teach a particular learner who arrives late every Tuesday morning. What might the range of explanations for this be?
> - They don't like my class.
> - They are tired because they are working late every Monday night due to lack of income.
> - They have to take their younger sibling to school first.
> - They can't afford to travel earlier as it's a more expensive train fare.
> - Every Monday night they stay at their Dad's house, and he doesn't get up early enough to get the learner to class on time.

6 Enhance verbal communication skills

This is an especially important reason for retaining your critical thinking lens. Communicating clearly and in a professional manner is important in any sector, but particularly so in an educational setting. This relates to **not only what you say but also how well you listen and respond.** So, often you might need to relay information to a colleague in a setting and this needs to be done in a precise way. This means recognizing that **in some settings everyday language is not precise enough**: consider for example, the difference between the remarks below, in a fictional conversation with a schoolteacher working with those in Reception (ages 4–5).

> 'There's a huge problem with SLCN in the class this year' – a generalization that uses imprecise language ('huge') and assumes knowledge of the acronym SLCN (Speech, Language and Communication Needs). Also, what might the word 'problem' mean here?

compared to the more precise and informative comment below:

> 'There's a small proportion of pupils who need additional support to meet expected standards in communication and language at the moment' – a much more precise and informative description of the situation.

7 Active and careful, mindful listening

This is also a core element of communication from a critical thinking position: often we need to listen to information which requires putting aside our own subjective beliefs or perspectives and being more open-minded. In practice, this might mean:

- reflecting back points someone is conveying to you to ensure you understand them;
- asking appropriate questions;
- being able to verbalize or present your own understanding or judgement on an issue.

> **TIP**
>
> It's also important to recognize that many other 'real-world' experiences you have while studying are opportunities that you can reflect upon and identify assets associated with these. Any kind of employment or volunteering is incredibly valuable, regardless of the role or setting. For example, all of the points identified in the section above about the reasons for critical thinking in settings are as relevant to the role of a customer service assistant in a retail setting as they are to a teacher in the early stages of their career.

How to handle it when things go wrong: the importance of critical reflection on a critical incident

Working with others – especially learners – often brings about unpredictable situations. When you're new to a setting, or role, it is common to feel uncertain, and it can be helpful to accept that we all make mistakes when we're learning and developing. In the same way that you would apply a compassionate mindset to young children who are learning a tricky skill such as putting on shoes or buttoning a cardigan, try to be kind and patient with yourself as you learn to work within the complexities of an educational environment.

When you make a mistake (because we all do), the best approach is to be honest, open, and remain professional: educational settings are centred around the concept of learning and self-development, and this culture and ethos is applicable to all. However difficult it may feel, **adopting a forward-looking mindset and thinking about how you will learn** from an experience is crucial – think back to the emphasis upon forward action in the previous chapter's reflective models we examined.

Similar to the models presented and discussed in the previous chapter, there are many variations on the basic idea, as in Figure 7.1.

You will make a positive impression upon your colleagues and manager(s) if the conversation you have with them following a mistake reflects the elements above. If you need to recount an incident, you might find using this basic template a good starting point, then return to Chapter 6 to further detail your reflection, understanding and ways forward.

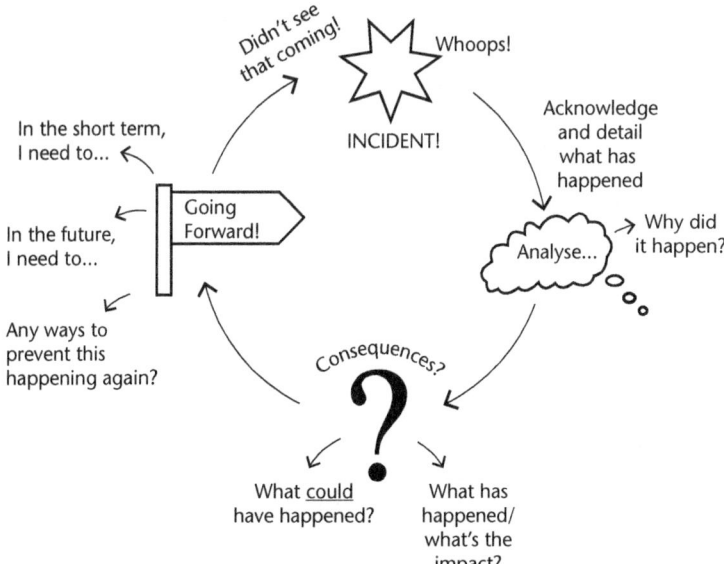

Figure 7.1 A variation on the reflective models

Also, remember that a critical incident might not be a negative experience: you might witness or be part of a very positive and impactful incident or occasion. It's just as worthwhile going through the same process as documented above, to identify what elements of the incident made it a success, and how a similar outcome might be achieved again in the future.

Critical thinking when considering career choices

Although it's common for graduates of Education to go into teaching, or careers supporting learners, there are two important points to bear in mind here: firstly, there are many other relevant career choices that can draw on your Education degree, and secondly, if you do want to pursue teaching, then drawing upon your critical thinking skills can help you to really think through this choice before you commit.

When considering future career paths, think back first to the idea and process of **reflection** and remember that **reflection is thinking about something, for a purpose**. While your professional life is likely to offer you many possibilities throughout its course, it's not advisable to leap into a particular role without giving this careful thought.

Critical thinking and self-enquiry can help you to identify aspects of yourself and your skills and then, in turn (using logic and reason), consider how well suited they might be to particular roles.

Many students of Education commence their undergraduate degree convinced that they want to progress to become a teacher. After experiences on placement and studying the education system in depth, this conviction may be strengthened (you want to be a teacher even more) or there may be uncertainty (no longer so sure).

What sources of information might influence you in making a decision about entering the teaching profession?

- Your experience as a learner: at school and in other settings
- Your experience in the classroom as an observer, or volunteer
- Conversations and insights gained from people you know who work in the education system
- Representations of teachers in different types of media
- Research from relevant organizations about the benefits of teaching as a career
- Your university careers service.

A key source of information here is also yourself. Honest and extensive critical self-reflection can help you with such a crucial decision. Some questions you might want to ask yourself, and discuss with others may include:

- Do I have a strong work ethic?
- Are my values aligned with pedagogical principles and the centrality of developing learners' potential?
- Do I thrive on variety, challenge and the unexpected?
- Am I motivated by the prospect of inspiring learners and making a difference to their lives?
- Can I work within a rigid system which might not always align with my ideals?
- Am I willing to commit to ongoing learning and training to stay up to date and continue lifelong professional development?
- Can I present information and communicate in an enthusiastic and engaging way?
- Do I have resilience to cope with emotionally demanding situations and periods of time? Or, can I commit to strategies to try and increase my resilience?
- Do I enjoy spending time with the age group I'm thinking of teaching?
- Can I be incredibly well organized and use my time well?
- Can I exercise patience, tolerance, empathy and understanding in my interactions with vulnerable learners?

Many would argue that teaching becomes a core part of the identity of those who work in the profession, and that it's unlikely to ever just be a 'job' that is easy to switch off from. This doesn't suit everyone, and can differ according to individuals' responsibilities and circumstances.

Take care with your research when trying to build up an accurate picture of what teaching is like as a career: providers of teacher training want to recruit you, and so their depiction of teaching will be different to others. Someone who has been teaching for thirty years may well have a different view to a recently qualified teacher.

Gathering plenty of views, having conversations with relevant individuals wherever you can, and considering this decision over a decent period of time (don't rush the decision) will help you to feel well informed with a balanced and realistic view of entering the teaching profession.

> **TIP**
>
> A credible source of advice about many components of teaching as a career is the UK graduate careers website, prospects.ac.uk. This website includes a career planner quiz which analyses your strengths and offers some potential matched job roles: https://www.prospects.ac.uk/planner.

Teaching critical thinking: the responsibility of nurturing developing minds

If you are considering a career that involves teaching, or working with learners in some capacity, then there's an added layer of thought and responsibility here; how do you role model yourself as a critical thinker, and how can opportunities for critical thinking be created across all stages and subjects? Lombardi et al.'s view is that 'No higher order skill will be more important for pupils to develop in the twenty-first century than critical thinking' (2024: 683), so it is important to be aware of this.

As adults, we are continually learning to navigate in a world awash with information, and this can be challenging. For learners with less life experience, greater vulnerabilities, and varying stages of cognitive development, the importance of fostering a critical thinking approach is crucial.

You may – even if you have diligently read every chapter preceding this – still not feel totally confident and certain about your own understanding of critical thinking, and how to implement this in the role of an educator. Jones (2024) suggests there are three viewpoints on this:

1 teaching critical thinking within a subject – in a discreet way
2 teaching critical thinking within a subject – in an explicit way
3 teaching critical thinking as a subject on its own.

Each approach has possibilities and problems, and a balanced strategy that seeks to incorporate and embed all three of these perspectives is likely to be most effective.

Remember: critical thinking is a concept, a mindset, an outlook and a habit – embedding this into young people's education can't be achieved in a quick lesson, a critical thinking assembly or week of activities, it needs to be threaded throughout their entire educational career. This means that in addition to using the term explicitly with learners and discussing the words and their meaning, it needs to be done in a way which is:

- frequent
- contextual
- relevant
- age and stage appropriate.

Opportunities to act in a critical thinking manner abound within every teaching and learning interaction. We nearly always have the possibility to consider another perspective, or to consider the logic behind an action or decision, but time and space in the curriculum and in day-to-day lessons can feel like a constraint to adding any other considerations to lesson plans. The important thing to bear in mind here is not to feel overwhelmed or daunted by the prospect of doing this – it really is something that will naturally occur as you develop professionally.

Some areas for action and opportunities to teach critical thinking might include:

- Any instance where a type of **media** is being used: who produced it, why, what is their motivation? Children and young people are often (quite rightly!) outraged when they think someone else is trying to control or persuade them to think in a certain way, and we know that many online platforms have algorithms designed to do just this, and that AI is only working to re-present what is already available. Children in the contemporary world receive so much of their information and understanding about the world via carefully curated (and sometimes manipulative) media sources, and as adults we are responsible for helping them to understand what is behind the media to enable them to 'decode the world' (Sperry and Scheibe, 2022: 3).
- Cherish the relationship between education and **freedom of thinking**, and the value that countless seminal educational thinkers have placed upon this. In your studies you may have come across the work of bell hooks, a prolific and very well-respected writer on issues of feminism, racism and social class. Her book *Teaching Critical Thinking: Practical Wisdom* reminds us that 'education [is] the surest route to freedom' (2009: 2). Freedom of thought for young people, and a growing awareness of others' thoughts in the world is a core philosophy to keep in your heart when you have taken on the role of teacher.
- **Let learners lead** where possible: oftentimes concepts such as children's rights or ownership of projects or activities begin with adult ideas and agenda, and so true participation and control by learners can become tokenistic. Children are the most divergent, creative and delightful free thinkers if the right conditions are created for them to

do so. Some classroom approaches that can help to stimulate these opportunities include plenty of discussion – led by learners – scenario- or problem-based learning, the creation of visual (rather than textual) resources, (supportive) peer 'judgement' and feedback, role play, use of graphic organizers (like mind maps or flow charts) or alignment with ideas along a continuum. There are lots of ideas around on teaching websites and blogs to help stimulate your ideas if you search for 'teaching critical thinking' (but be sure to apply your critical lens to the information you find!).

Keep looking through your critical lenses: professional development

Any kind of professional role brings with it an expectation that you will be committed to your profession's principles and values, and hold the best interests of your learners, or service users, in mind. There are some habits and approaches you can adopt that will enable you to do this, which we outline below.

1 **Keep up to date** with credible sources of information and changes in your field or line of work, for example, access relevant news items, professional publications, blogs from high profile individuals in your area, and subscribe to policy updates. Issues in society, technology, the economy or politics can swiftly impact upon the educational sector and impact upon both professionals and learners.
2 Don't neglect the importance of **networking, talking and sharing** with others you are learning with and working alongside. Making and keeping contact with people who have had similar experiences or work in the same area as you can be hugely beneficial, even though you might not know it yet. Introduce yourself to people on training courses, on placement, chat about your specific experiences and area of interest, and connect via social media or whatever kind of platform works best in your area (e.g. LinkedIn). The careers website Prospects (www.prospects.ac.uk) has some great advice on using social media for job hunting and developing your own 'brand' i.e. your outward-facing professional persona. Don't underestimate the impact of your online footprint and presence upon your reputation and job prospects.
3 Try to avoid echo chambers: if you choose to only surround yourself with people like you, who have had the same experiences, and hold the same beliefs, a critical lens can be lost. Your critical thinking will

be enhanced by choosing to **proactively place yourself in new, different situations with people and ideas you may not be familiar with**. Try to mindfully engage with diverse experiences and people so that you continue to learn from different cultures, perspectives and traditions.

Critical thinking is also an element to bring into your opportunities for structured **career development**. There are ways you can try to make this habitual, by adopting the identity of a critical thinker who is committed to self-enquiry and personal development. For example:

- During appraisals or progress meetings with a manager: particularly if you're putting forward a case for support with development in your role.
- While having career conversations (formal or informal) with colleagues.
- Seeking out mentoring and coaching – some organizations offer this, others don't. If not, consider asking if there are opportunities. It's worth doing a bit of research (this includes asking around) into what might be available to you.
- Sharing ideas – being courageous to do this. Don't be afraid when you are asked for your view – or even when you are not! Usually, colleagues or those in leadership positions are keen to hear ideas from the perspectives of others, and you might be surprised at how productive and positive a quick conversation can be with someone more experienced or senior.

The role of critical thinking for inclusion

Whatever career path you follow, particularly if you are entering the world of education, recognizing and valuing differences amongst learners is fundamental. Practitioners bring with them their own lived experiences, assumptions and biases, and acknowledging these and reflecting upon them is vital.

Any education setting is a diverse place and so reflective critical thinking will help you to have greater awareness of how your own experiences or assumptions might impact upon your reaction to a particular event, or the way you interact with someone.

Learners' needs and experiences may differ for many reasons, including but not limited to their age, gender, ethnicity, religion or belief, disability, language, sexuality, socio-economic background, caring responsibilities, culture, nationality, or previous life experiences which could include trauma. Thinking critically and reflectively about the possible reasons for a learner's levels of engagement, behaviour or communication with empathy and an open mind will lead to better connections, and an improved learning experience for all those involved. You might behave more inclusively, for example, by not making assumptions about others' experiences or capabilities, realizing that some knowledge about norms and practices may be new to others, taking care with language, and realizing that every small action you take to include one colleague or learner tends to improve the experience for everyone.

Summing up

Critical thinking in practice as you transition into an employment role has the potential to transform your experience, personal development, and the quality of learners' experiences. Taking your critical thinking mindset into all kinds of employment or placement experiences will enable you to project a professional and committed persona to employers and colleagues and will assist you in embedding core values of inquiry, inclusion and ongoing development into all that you do. Keep your commitment to critical thinking at the forefront of your professional practice and be proud of yourself for carrying this into all that you do, and potentially into the next generation of critical thinkers.

References

hooks, b. (2009), *Teaching Critical Thinking: Practical Wisdom*, New York: Routledge.

Jones, A. (2024), *Critical Thinking in Schools: Can it be Taught, and How?* Available at: Available at: https://www.sec-ed.co.uk/content/best-practice/critical-thinking-in-schools-can-it-be-taught-and-how (accessed 22 October 2024).

Lombardi, L., Thomas, V., Rodeyns, J., Mednick, F. J., De Backer, F. and Lombaerts, K. (2021), 'Primary School Teachers' Experiences of Teaching Strategies that Promote Pupils' Critical Thinking', *Educational Studies*, 50 (5): 683–701. Available at: https://doi.org/10.1080/03055698.2021.1990017 (accessed 7 May 2025).

Sperry, C. and Scheibe, C. (2022), *Teaching Students to Decode the World: Media Literacy and Critical Thinking Across the Curriculum*, Alexandria, VA: Association for Supervision and Curriculum Development.

Signposts to resources

To help with your ongoing professional development and lifelong critical thinking:
Squiggly careers: www.amazingif.com
Information about mentoring and coaching: 'Coaching and Mentoring: Definitions, Differences and Uses'. Available at: https://uk.indeed.com/career-advice/career-development/coaching-and-mentoring-definitions
Carol Dweck, growth mindset TED talk: Carol Dweck, 'The Power of Believing that You can Improve'. Available at: https://www.ted.com/talks/carol_dweck_the_power_of_believing_that_you_can_improve?language=en (accessed 7 May 2025).

Critical Thinking Glossary

There are a range of words, concepts or ideas that are often referred to when we discuss critical thinking, the most common of which we have identified and defined below. It is useful if you have an understanding of these terms, as many are used in pieces of research that you will come across.

Feel free to add any more words with their definitions that you come across or annotate this glossary by writing definitions in your own words.

academic literature Texts that are written by academics. This type of text is often peer reviewed before publication.
anchoring bias, or effect The influence of your starting point when you are beginning to consider an argument, or position. This initial point of view may then influence your subsequent judgements, and the evidence you are willing to consider when researching an argument.
argument A collection of perspectives or points which form together to present a particular position on an issue. A core part of an argument is the reasoning and evidence as to how the conclusion, or judgement, has been arrived at.
artificial intelligence (AI) The use of technological tools or systems to generate output that would usually require human effort. In academic contexts, this is usually in relation to the generation of ideas (often passages of writing) via the internet or other specific websites. At the time of writing this book, the most common types of AI under discussion in universities include Grammarly, ChatGPT and Quilbot, but new tools are emerging at a rapid rate as technology develops.

In a teaching and learning context, the use of AI holds many possibilities to assist teachers and learners, and help to create new resources. However, most universities have very clear guidance about the extent to which they permit the use of AI in assessed work, so be sure to check your assessment regulations, as inappropriate use of AI can result in academic misconduct, or plagiarism. There is a useful insight into the use of AI from a student's point of view on the BBC website here: www.bbc.com/news/articles/cz04emrxp4xo.amp?utm_source=substack&utm_medium=email
assertion A claim or statement being put forward e.g. 'the writer asserts that ...'
bias An inclination to align, or side, with a particular point of view. This may then be represented, disproportionately in the information produced.
claim The position or standpoint within an argument.

confirmation bias This is the – very natural – tendency of most human beings to prefer to accept or align themselves with viewpoints they come across that already resemble their own, rather than seeking out new information that might challenge these beliefs.

correlation This refers to the relationship identified between variables (or factors), usually in regard to statistical data, but the term may also be used to illustrate connections more broadly without specific reference to quantitative data e.g. lecturers observe a correlation between students' attendance and their attainment.

credibility The extent to which we find something to be convincing, or believable – or not. It can also carry connotations of an individual (such as an author of an information source) being respected or expert in their area.

critical analysis This is the act of breaking an issue down into its component parts and examining the various aspects. Remember, 'critical' doesn't mean criticizing, but the best critical analysis is applied when we systematically scrutinize and weigh up the various parts of an argument or issue, in order to arrive at a well-informed and balanced judgement, or conclusion.

critical incident An event or instance in the workplace that usually has a significant impact and requires inquiry and reflection.

critical reflection Engaging in purposeful thinking about a situation, circumstance or event, with the view to a particular forward-looking outcome – often to change a behaviour in the future.

deductive Often paired up with *inductive* (see below), both of which frequently appear alongside the word 'reasoning'. In its simplest sense, deductive thinking means thinking logically and coming to a conclusion based on key premises or ideas. For example, the most common feature within an education system is the presence of a teacher. Schools are part of the education system. Therefore, teachers are a common feature of schools. In regards to undertaking research involving data collection, a deductive approach would require beginning with a belief (or conclusion) and then looking for data (often with an experimental approach) to try and substantiate or support this.

echo chamber Any kind of setting (online or face to face) where the same, usually limited pool of ideas are repeated and reinforced without significant attempts to look for any counter views or alternative evidence. These can perpetuate some ideas and distort reality for those within them.

elucidate To explain further and elaborate upon a point in order to make it clear.

empirical Usually used alongside the term 'evidence', or to describe a type of research study. If evidence or a finding is referred to as 'empirical', it means it has been developed as a result of observing and documenting specific phenomena or experiences. For example, you may be asked to find a journal article on a particular topic, and be advised that it should be about a piece of empirical research rather than a written review of literature in that area.

enquiry This is the act of seeking out information. You may also see this referred to in American sources as 'inquiry'. We might talk about having an 'enquiring mind'.

epistemology Concerned with knowledge: what we consider to be knowledge, how we come to know this, and limitations. From a research perspective, our epistemological belief influences choices a researcher may make about what they believe to be the best ways of researching that particular phenomena, or type of reality in their circumstances. When thinking about how researchers make decisions about how they should gather data, traditional social research ideas advise that firstly, researchers should be certain of their ontological viewpoint on that issue, or area they are examining. This then impacts upon their epistemological approach in terms of how they believe valid knowledge can be generated in regards to that issue. Consequently, a researcher then considers the most appropriate methodological approach (e.g. whether quantitative or qualitative methods would be best), and lastly, what data collection tools (e.g. an interview, or questionnaire) will align best with these beliefs, their research question, and their participants, or sample.

evaluation This is the process of examining information and making assessments about an issue, then deciding upon a conclusion or judgement. In educational research, an evaluation is often concerned with undertaking systematic enquiry into a specific phenomenon (such as a classroom intervention or strategy) and gathering data about its impact. For example, a teacher might begin a new method or programme to teach a particular mathematical concept, and they could assess pupils' knowledge of that concept with a test before using the new programme, then repeat the test afterwards (sometimes referred to as pre- and post-testing). The results – hopefully an improved measurement – would evaluate the programme's impact. Evaluation can also occur from a qualitative (non-numerical) perspective, by asking people for their views of something after their experiences.

explicit To make something very apparent and clear, at the forefront of an argument. If something is explicit there is no confusion or vagueness about what is being presented.

fallacy This is a word to describe a mistaken or incorrect belief that has been based on unsound arguments or evidence. A fallacy uses some kind of flawed reasoning that may not be easy to spot in an argument. There are various types of fallacies if you look further into some of the ideas behind this term, see Chatfield (2018).

grey literature This refers to information sources produced by organizations that are not usually academic (peer reviewed) or commercial, but is worthwhile considering in your research, once you have carefully scrutinized their qualities. Examples of grey literature include reports from relevant organizations (e.g. charities), a government white paper or statistics, and a policy document.

hypothesis This is a belief statement that is usually associated with the objective of a piece of research. For example, 'my hypothesis is that students will receive higher grades in their assignments if they have read this book on critical thinking'. There is as yet an unknown claim, and an associated explanation or consequence the claimant thinks might occur as a result of the phenomena they are examining.

implicit It can be helpful to think of this as almost the opposite of explicit (above). If a message or idea in a source is implicit, it's not necessarily easy to see; it may be implied or suggested, but not stated directly. We might claim that an idea is 'implicit' in a piece of work if it's something we have identified as a result of 'reading between the lines'.

inductive Often placed in opposition to 'deductive' reasoning (above), taking an inductive approach means that we generate ideas from an open starting point, and the conclusions we draw are led by the data that is produced from a research project.

interpret Explaining the meaning of something, usually information. For example, we may need to interpret the meaning or key messages behind a set of statistics.

interrogation To question and examine evidence, or an argument.

logical reasoning The relationship between the claim being made and the reason(s) presented to support the claim.

objective Usually considered to be the opposite of 'subjective' (see below). An objective point of view is one that is usually considered to be impartial, and not biased or influenced by personal or individual feelings or factors.

ontology A belief about the nature of social reality, and what really exists in the world, sometimes referred to as a 'world view'. You may come across references to 'ontological' assumptions or an 'ontological stance' which refers to the fundamental, or core, beliefs that a person may hold about aspects of reality. When looking at empirical research, 'ontology' is often featured alongside 'epistemology' (see above), as they are both essential foundations to social research.

peer review A process where academics/experts in related topic areas read and comment on each other's writing. This usually happens before texts are accepted and published.

provenance The source or origin of something.

reasoning The process through which an issue is considered in a logical manner, often involving the consideration of varying arguments, which are then retained or rejected.

recency bias An inclination to align with, or believe in, a particular point of view because it is recent, and you are more likely to recall it easily.

reflective practice Purposefully thinking through and evaluating our own actions, or practice (often in a professional setting) and identifying actions to implement leading from this reflection.

reliability Used largely in relation to quantitative (numerical) research, a study is considered to be reliable if the 'test' (data collection tool) can be used consistently (and get similar results) in a different setting, with a different sample.

rhetoric This is the practice of presenting information to persuade someone. You may hear of 'rhetorical writing', utilizing persuasive language in a text.

sample A selection of people featured as participants in research. Samples are used as it's not possible to conduct research on everyone.

subjective Usually considered to be the opposite of 'objective'. A point of view, argument, or person can be said to be subjective if what they are presenting is an individual, personal (possibly biased) perspective that doesn't take into account other pieces of relevant information or evidence.

synthesis Bringing together and combining different elements e.g. different ideas, different reading about an educational topic.

thesis statement One or two sentences that outline the main topic, what will be discussed and how it will be discussed.

unconscious bias A distorted or unbalanced viewpoint, belief or perspective that is not always explicitly known to the holder. It is a concept often associated with the views people hold of those in a population group different to themselves, for example based on ethnicity or social class, which can then lead to stereotypes and result in discriminatory behaviour.

validity The word 'valid' is associated with ideas of quality and rigour (how thoroughly something has been done). In relation to empirical research where data is being gathered, validity is a concept used to make a type of assessment as to whether the research has captured or measured what it actually set out to do. It is often used in conjunction with *reliability* (see above) as a criteria to judge the quality of research.

well-balanced Ensuring that all sides of the argument are provided and there is not just a focus on one. A well-balanced argument or perspective would not be subjective or biased.

My own additional definitions:

Critical Thinking Sentence Starters and Other Language Tools

One important way we can demonstrate greater critical thinking in our work is through our use of language. This includes the style, tone and choice of words, all of which can impact significantly upon the extent to which a piece of work conveys critical thinking.

We encourage you to take these ideas as a starting point and develop your own phrases and expressions, but the lists below are a useful starting point to give you a few initial ideas. It is important to try and add variety in the language you use within your written work (i.e. not always using the same phrases such as, 'another point of view is … ') and so having a toolbox of appropriate phrases to draw upon can be valuable.

Beginning a piece of work – phrases to use in an introduction

- This work examines …
- The focus of this assignment is upon …
- Within this essay, ideas around XXX are analysed …
- The key aspect discussed within this work centres around …
- Views from XXX are examined and then linked to …
- The practice of XXX will be explored and evaluated …

Introducing ideas from literature …

- As [author's surname] has challenged …
- Drawing on [author's surname] we can explore …
- One such assertion amongst the literature is that of XX [author]
- The work of XX [author] suggests that …
- A common theme within the literature is that of …
- This issue is represented within the literature in various ways …

- Studies exploring this area tend to emphasize ...
- Numerous studies have identified the issue of ...

Presenting a new perspective or issue
- This next section argues that ...
- Another area for consideration is ...
- Firstly, views around XXX will be examined, followed by ...
- In comparison, another viewpoint to consider is ...

Comparing findings of studies: highlighting differences
- While some research has identified ... other studies have noted ....
- A contrast in findings is apparent between ...

Comparing findings of studies: highlighting similarities
- Other studies, such as XX, confirm this ...
- The importance of this issue has been consistently highlighted amongst literature ...

Use of hedging
Generally, the key with hedging language is to express caution and avoid making generalizations. A key part of this is avoiding definitive, or absolute, language because this shows that our viewpoint is open to a wider range of perspectives.

A useful way to think about hedging language is to consider the opposite of what might be a definitive or sweeping statement, as some of the examples below illustrate:

Definitive claim	Hedging claim
Excluded pupils will ...	Excluded pupils may ...
These findings prove that ...	These findings suggest that ...
Teachers will ...	Teachers might ...
A consequence of this is ...	A consequence of this could be ...

Other such cautious phrases include:
- It is reasonable to suggest that ...
- It could be perceived as ....
- Arguably, this evidence could show that ...
- While there is limited evidence to support this viewpoint wholly, ...

Identifying limitations with existing sources
- The study's findings should be viewed with caution due to ...
- It should be noted that this study is limited due to ...
- The main weakness of this study relates to ...
- However, this research does not take into account ...

Highlighting strengths of previous studies
- The strengths of previous research are ...
- A positive aspect of this research is ...
- Existing studies have contributed ...

Highlighting weaknesses of previous studies
- Previous research has not discussed ...
- In studies focusing on [topic] there is limited discussion about ...
- Existing research fails to consider ...

Ending your work, or bringing a section to a close: synthesizing and summing up
- It is apparent that ...
- Discussions in this work have highlighted that ...
- Having taken into account ...
- In summary,
- In bringing together these discussions,
- To conclude the analysis presented within this work ...
- The evidence presented and reviewed in this assignment presents ...

A key source we always recommend to students here to further develop academic writing is the University of Manchester's Academic Phrasebank: https://www.phrasebank.manchester.ac.uk/

Reference

Chatfield, T. (2018), *Critical Thinking*, London: SAGE Publications.

Index

academic writing 57, 59, 68, 69, 70, 75, 78, 136
action planning 97, 98
analysis, critical 14, 15, 52
artificial intelligence (AI) 26, 28, 44
arguments 58
  constructing 45–7
  identifying flaws 12, 36
  maps/mapping 49, 102, 124
  viewpoint(s) 1, 5, 9, 10, 11, 29, 32, 33, 50, 51, 58, 61, 74, 80, 130
articulation 86, 88
assessment 7, 35–7, 39, 44, 50–3, 69, 79, 82, 83, 85, 103, 129
  formative 53
  summative 53
audience 23, 50, 69, 82–9
  participation 87
authenticity 27
author(s)/creator of a source 22, 23, 26, 28, 29, 35, 39–43, 61, 63, 64, 68, 130, 134

bias 23, 32
  types of 33
bibliographic information 38, 39, 49, 55, 63, 65
Bloom's Taxonomy 12–14
Boud, David 94, 95, 97, 98, 108–11
Bronfenbrenner, Urie 5
Brookfield, Stephen 100, 110, 111

capabilities xi, 54, 126
careers 64, 68, 120, 122, 124
chronosystem 5

communication xii, 54, 79, 81–7, 89, 118
  spoken (verbal) 79, 81–87, 89
  written xii, 79, 81, 82, 84, 86, 89
conclusions 67, 84, 87, 97, 98
confidence xii, 30, 35, 46, 51, 68, 69, 71, 80, 88, 89
credibility
  of arguments 48
critical thinking 17–19, 21, 24, 30, 31, 34–7, 39–41, 44, 45, 48, 49, 52, 53, 55, 57, 58–60, 63, 67, 70, 74, 75, 79, 81, 83, 84, 88, 89, 92, 103, 112, 115–118, 120, 122–6
  definitions 2, 18
  quiz 17
critical questions 16, 17
critical reading 28, 39, 45, 57, 59

description 11, 12, 15
Dewey, John 92, 95
direct quotations 39, 61, 63–5, 75

employability ix, 54, 115
  employers 115, 126
  employability skills 115–16
epistemology 29
evaluation 9, 12, 21, 42, 58, 94, 95, 97, 110, 131
evidence ix, ixx, 2, 9, 10, 12, 16, 18, 21, 28, 33, 34, 35, 37, 40, 45, 47, 48, 57–60, 63, 64, 68, 69, 74, 75, 84, 87, 88, 102, 103, 116, 117, 129, 135, 136

137

Index

Gibbs, Graham 97, 98, 109–12
group work 54

imposter syndrome 69, 70
incident, critical 118–20
inclusion 125-26
information 64, 65, 69, 70, 85, 86, 117, 118, 121, 124,
    sources of 21–3, 25–6
    consumption of ix, 35
introductions 67

Kolb, David 95–8

logic 4, 34, 123
    logical flow 61, 77

media 1, 5, 7, 9, 18, 2 7, 47, 48, 50, 78, 102, 120, 123, 124
    news sources 8
    social media 1, 8, 26
macrosystem 5–7
mesosystem 5
microsystem 5

objectivity 23
observations, *see also* journals, diaries in practice 11, 96, 103, 109
ontology 29
opinions xii, 1, 5, 7, 9–11, 32–34, 54, 69
    versus informed viewpoints 5, 9, 10, 34
oral presentations 89

pace 73, 82, 86, 88
paraphrasing 63–6
peer review 25
persuasion 81, 83, 123, 133
Piaget, Jean 95
placement, or work-based practice 6, 16, 103, 104–5, 116–18
plagiarism, academic misconduct, collusion 38, 65, 72
post-graduate/further study 13, 70

productivity 71–3
professional development x, 124–25

qualitative 29–31, 34
quantitative 29–31, 43, 116
quotations 61

reading 1, 16, 21, 27, 28, 37, 39, 45, 50–53, 57–59, 64, 73, 75
    (*see also* consumption) 21
references 38
    referencing viii, 38, 39
reflection 91–3
    reflective practice 101
    models of 93–101
reliability (and validity) 30-1

Schön, Donald 92, 99,
skills viii, 13, 54, 67, 88, 115, 117
sources ix, 8, 10, 45, 49, 50, 51, 53, 55, 57–9, 64
    types of 10, 23, 24, 37
authenticity 27, 47
space 49
    organisation 37–9
    analysis of 50–4
Stenhouse, Lawrence 3
structuring work and arguments viii, 59
    Structuring presentations 84
subjectivity 57
summarizing 63, 64

teaching xii, 44, 80, 100
    as a career 120–1
    teaching critical thinking 122–4
theory, learning theories 15
tone xii, 68, 75, 82, 83, 86, 88

validity (and reliability) 30, 31
visual representation 12, 95
voice 67, 69
    academic 40, 64
Vygotsky 79, 95,

writing, critically 70, 71
writing groups 71, 72